IN DEFENCE
OF HANSLICK

By

STEWART DEAS

Revised edition
with a new preface

1972

GREGG INTERNATIONAL PUBLISHERS
LIMITED

ISBN 0 576 28242 1
First edition 1940
Second edition published in 1972 by
Gregg International Publishers Limited
Westmead, Farnborough, Hants,England.

Printed in offset by Franz Wolf,Heppenheim/Bergstrasse
Western Germany

PREFACE

ALTHOUGH this edition is largely a reprint of the original publication, I have taken the opportunity to make one or two minor corrections and additions. The original last chapter has been discarded and replaced by one more in keeping with present-day acceptance of Hanslick's work as an important part of the documentation of his period. Indeed, if I were writing a book about Hanslick now I doubt whether it would occur to me to give it a title including the words "in defence". But in the earlier years of this century there seemed to be so much ill-informed and abusive writing about the man, that I had to make my position clear at the outset.

The past thirty years have seen a revival of interest in the principles of criticism and problems of aesthetics. They have seen, for example, the founding of the British Society of Aesthetics, and the appearance of an increasing number of books and articles devoted to the discussion of artistic criteria. The creative artists themselves have been, for better or worse, unusually vocal about their aims and procedures. In music, no less than in the other arts, there has been a great deal of "Composition as Explanation" or *vice versa*, if I may recall a now forgotten title of Gertrude Stein. Hanslick, I think, would have been highly amused by it all but, as one always most concerned with the work of his contemporaries, he would have searched for the gold amidst so much dross, and scarified with his witty pen those who sought to bolster up feeble achievement with pretentious theories.

As far as his own work is concerned, no better proof of its vitality and importance for the history of 19th century music could be provided than the reissue of the English edition of *Vom Musikalisch-Schönen* ("The Beautiful in Music" The Library of Liberal Arts, 1957) and the publication of a selection of his criticism under the title "Vienna's Golden Years of Music" translated and edited by Henry Pleasants (New York 1950, London 1951). But more recently still, it has been found possible to republish the whole of his collected works in the original German (Gregg International Publishers Ltd. 1970), a fact which surely testifies to their scholarly value and permanent historical interest.

If this little book can in any way claim to have contributed to these later developments I am more than amply rewarded. In the many favourable reviews which greeted its first appearance in a wartime England, I was most heartened by one simple sentence in *The Times Literary Supplement*: "Mr. Deas has shown the way to approach the criticism of the past". If I did, it was almost inadvertently, but perhaps more writers in those days needed to be shown the way.

S.D.
Froxfield
Hampshire
1972.

CONTENTS

It is only an auctioneer who can equally and impartially admire all schools of art.—Oscar Wilde.

IN DEFENCE OF HANSLICK

CHAPTER I

EARLY YEARS

"HANSLICK was, in fact, the most colossal ignoramus and charlatan that has ever succeeded in imposing himself on an editor as a musical critic." [1]

"I have read Hanslick's collected works patiently without discovering either in his patronage of Brahms or in his attacks on Wagner, Verdi, Bruckner, the early works of Beethoven, Palestrina's *Stabat Mater*, or any other work a little off the average Viennese concert-goer's track in 1880, any knowledge of anything whatever." [2]

These two quotations may perhaps be somewhat extreme to be taken as representative of the prevailing attitude of musicians to the writings of Eduard Hanslick, but they contain in concentrated form the kind of criticism which is only too frequently met with, particularly in the hundreds of books that have been written about Wagner. The first quotation is taken from a whole chapter devoted to condemnation of Hanslick and based on the writings of two German writers, Max Morold and Wilhelm Kienzl, both of

[1] Ernest Newman, *Fact and Fiction about Wagner*, p. 31.
[2] Sir Donald Tovey, *Essays in Musical Analysis*, Vol. 2, p. 70.

whom are too manifestly Wagnerian to be taken seriously even if their remarks could really be borne out by reference to Hanslick's work. The second quotation is the kernel of a paragraph which contains, among other remarks, the statement that Hanslick's general and musical culture was of the type which "does not dream of revising a first impression."

One of the chief drawbacks to a true appreciation of Hanslick's work on the part of English readers is the fact that of all the dozen or so close packed volumes of his collected writings, only one[1] has found its way into English, the famous *Vom Musikalisch-Schönen.* It is indeed hardly to be wondered at that the masses of concert notices and occasional articles of which the other volumes, with the exception of two volumes of autobiography, consist, should have remained untranslated, as their interest is often purely topical. But it is surprising that those who have examined even a few of the books in the original German should fail to be impressed by the conscientious thoroughness which characterizes Hanslick's work and the frequent proof of a mind by no means finally "made up" or closed to contemporary ideas. It will be my endeavour in these pages to put before the English reader the real Hanslick as he emerges from his own words, to indicate particularly the lesser known aspects of his criticism and the origin and development of his famous theory of "The Beautiful in Music," and to

[1] Since this was written a selection of passages from the collected edition has appeared in English under the title *Vienna's Golden Years of Music 1850-1900* ed. Henry Pleasants (New York 1950, Simon & Schuster; London 1951, Gollancz).

remove as far as I can the dross of so much Wagnerian criticism which has too long obscured what is vital and admirable in his work.

Hanslick was born in Prague on September 11th, 1825. In the first sentence of his autobiography (*Aus meinem Leben*) he tells us that he had "the inestimable good fortune to be able to look back on a serene and happy childhood and to think of his parents never otherwise than with the greatest affection and gratitude." His father, of peasant origin, had embarked at first on a course in Theology at Prague, but, after a year or two, in a disillusioned frame of mind, took to philosophy and æsthetics on which he later lectured at the Prague Hochschule. As a young man, to eke out his scanty pay as "Scriptor" at the University Library, Hanslick's father gave pianoforte lessons and, having had the good luck to buy the winning ticket in a forty-thousand gulden lottery, found himself in a position to marry one of his most attractive pupils who became the mother of two daughters and three sons. Eduard was the middle son, and his general education up to University entrance was given to him, as to his brothers and sisters, by his father who, as the result of a severe illness, had to give up his library duties and devoted most of his time to his family.[1] Over a number of years Hanslick's

[1] His father's luck and misfortune both find an interesting echo in a sentence of Hanslick's *Vom Musikalisch-Schönen*

father compiled a *History and Description of the Library of the University of Prague*, which was published in 1851 as a result of a grant in aid by the *Akademie der Wissenschaften* of Vienna.

From his mother Hanslick inherited a love for the theatre and a predilection for French literature. This is a fact which is worth noting at the outset because it explains to a great extent, I think, the cast of mind exhibited in a great deal of Hanslick's subsequent writing about opera.

Description and criticism of operas does in fact occupy a very large proportion of Hanslick's literary output, and his early formed ideas as to the nature of opera, as to what is true "theatre" and what is not, remained with him throughout his strenuous warfare against the music of Wagner and his followers. The first opera he heard was Mozart's "Magic Flute" and the first play Schiller's "William Tell." His mother took out two subscription tickets for the Prague Theatre and took her children in turn to both plays and operas. "The deepest musical impression of my youth," he says, "I received from opera. No concert music could compare, in its effect on me, with 'Der Freischütz.' An uncanny bliss, a heavenly shuddering

(Eng. trans., p. 26): "Music may undoubtedly awaken feelings of great joy or intense sorrow; but might not the same or a still greater effect be produced by the news that we have won the first prize in the lottery, or by the dangerous illness of a friend?"

prevented me from sleeping for a long time after such a performance and the first thing I did on awakening was to recall at the keyboard the enchanting melodies." Other operas which he speaks of as having had an early and strong effect on him were Spohr's "Jessonda"[1] and "Faust," Marschner's "Hans Heiling" and "Templer und Jüdin" and Meyerbeer's "Les Huguenots." Compared with these works he admits that in early years Mozart's operas seemed "tame and outmoded." Only later did Mozart's greatness become clear to him. Beethoven's "Fidelio" he knew at that time only through the pianoforte score, as it was not performed at Prague, whose repertoire from 1835–1845 also failed to include any of Gluck's operas. This omission was the occasion of Hanslick's first literary effort. Through some of his friends Hanslick was approached by the editor of a journal called *Ost und West* with a view to his contributing music criticism, and this, not without some misgivings on his father's part, he agreed to do. He describes charmingly his anxiety as he awaited the appearance of his first notice. "Only those who have experienced it themselves, know the feverish expectation, somewhere between anxiety and bliss, with which one waits to see oneself in print for the first time. It was on a December evening in 1844 and I walked up and down for a good half-hour before the newspaper office opened, and I was able to receive my

---

[1] This was also a favourite opera of Brahms.

first concert-notice." But its reception brought a disappointment; about two-thirds of the article had been cut by the editor. The concert had included a performance of the Finale from Gluck's "Armide," and Hanslick in his youthful zeal had complained of the absence of such a work from the Prague Theatre's repertoire, comparing the concert performance to a meeting of the early Christians who were forced to hold their services in secret in the catacombs. The passage was ruled out as an allusion to religion, a forbidden topic!

Hanslick was then nineteen years old and had become a student of law at the University, but he took his duties as a critic very seriously from the first. "I did not judge any composition without both before and after the performance reading it or playing it through on the piano—a habit to which I have remained faithful till the present day, that is to say, for about fifty years." This statement, and others throughout his writings, should be sufficient to refute the remarks of one Max Morold, quoted by Ernest Newman,[1] that "Hanslick seems to have been able neither to hear harmonies nor to read notes," if indeed such extravagant remarks are worthy of serious notice. There is considerable evidence that Hanslick was an accomplished pianist. For four years he had pianoforte and theory lessons from

[1] In *Fact and Fiction about Wagner*.

Tomascheck, "one hour weekly for pianoforte and two hours weekly for harmony, counterpoint, instrumentation and composition." Tomascheck was a highly respected teacher and had some reputation as a composer in his day. His vivid recollection of the playing of Beethoven,[1] whom he first heard in Prague in 1798, must have been a particular source of inspiration to his pupils. But he seems to have been a somewhat tyrannical master and his real musical sympathies lay earlier than Beethoven. In view of Hanslick's statement that Tomascheck's lessons were quite devoid of any historical or æsthetic considerations, one sentence in Tomascheck's summing up of Beethoven as a composer seems strange. "Harmony, counterpoint, eurythm, and particularly musical æsthetics, he did not seem to have overmuch at heart. . . ." The foundation of Tomascheck's pianoforte teaching, according to Hanslick, was Bach's "Das Wohltemperierte Klavier." Other works studied were Beethoven's Sonatas (except the later ones), Tomascheck's own Rhapsodies and Sonatas, all the studies of Thalberg, Chopin and Henselt, and some of Liszt's works. He insisted on all his pupils playing not only solos but also duets from memory, an unusual accomplishment for his or even for a later day. Hanslick's usual partner in these duets was

[1] Quoted in part by Thayer and more fully in *Beethoven— Impressions of Contemporaries* (O.U.P., 1927).

Julius Schulhoff, later a celebrated virtuoso pianist, whose place, when he left Prague, was taken by Ambros, the famous music historian. Ambros and Hanslick became intimate friends, although their enthusiasms were not altogether the same. Hanslick was ten years younger than Ambros, but the similarity of their lives—both being torn between their professional studies of law and their innate enthusiasm for music—gave them a strong bond in common and led to a lively interchange of letters when for some years they were separated. Ambros wrote on musical events for a journal called *Bohemia*, and so Hanslick in his first journalistic work had the joy and advantage of Ambros's constant companionship as a colleague.

The most noteworthy event of their time together in Prague was the visit of Berlioz in 1846, when he gave a succession of concerts there. Hanslick tells us Berlioz was practically unknown in Prague except to a select few who, like Ambros and himself, kept in touch with the most recent musical developments by reading Schumann's *Neue Zeitschrift für Musik*. To such young enthusiasts the piano-duet arrangement of the "King Lear" Overture and Liszt's pianoforte version of the "Sinfonie fantastique" were well known. Hanslick introduced Berlioz to his master Tomascheck, whose name and works were up to that time quite unknown to him. Berlioz in his *Memoirs* mentions a visit to one of Tomascheck's concerts of his own (Tomascheck's) compositions, but he does not mention Hanslick, although a good deal of space is devoted to Ambros. Hanslick says Berlioz's only remark on leaving Tomascheck after his first visit was, "Il a l'air bien enchanté de lui-même." It seems likely that Berlioz's omission of any mention of Hanslick was intentional, as Hanslick himself points out that his later criticisms of Berlioz's works, not so unqualified in their praise as the early ones, were badly taken by the composer. At a later date (1866) when Berlioz visited Vienna to conduct his "Damnation de Faust" no actual meeting took place between the two men, although Hanslick was present at a banquet in Berlioz's honour and had visited him a few years earlier in Paris. But when Hanslick went to Vienna in 1846 to complete the fourth and last year of his law studies at the University, he went armed with a letter of introduction from Berlioz to Ernst and to Liszt.

CHAPTER II

HANSLICK AND WAGNER

TWO short meetings with Wagner and one with Schumann preceded Hanslick's student year in Vienna. The remarks made by the two composers about each other as reported by him are typical of the impression they made. Schumann, who lent Hanslick the newly finished score of "Tannhäuser" to study, on being asked if he had any dealings with Wagner, said, "No. For me Wagner is impossible; he is undoubtedly a gifted man, but he never stops talking. One simply can't always be talking." Wagner's first conversation with Hanslick (in Marienbad in 1845) had been constantly disturbed by the screeches of the composer's parrot to which, however, Wagner confessed himself to be quite accustomed. When Hanslick renewed his acquaintance in Dresden the following year Wagner began to speak about Schumann, with whom he claimed he was outwardly on good terms. "But," he said, "one can't have dealings with Schumann; he's an impossible fellow; he never talks at all."

Hanslick's first literary work in Vienna consisted of a series of articles in the *Weiner Musikzeitung* on Wagner's "Tannhäuser," which he first heard performed under the composer's direction at Dresden in

1846. It had not yet reached Vienna, and in fact was not to be performed there until 1859. These analytical articles of Hanslick were the occasion of Wagner's one long letter [1] to him, part of which is worth reproducing here:

"What separates you by a world from me is your high opinion of Meyerbeer. I say that with complete candour because I am his personal friend and have every reason to value him as a colleague and amiable man. But when I consider everything in the making of operatic music which shows inner carelessness and outward laboriousness, it is summed up in the conception 'Meyerbeer,' and all the more so because I recognize in Meyerbeer's music great skill in external effectiveness which impedes the noble maturity of art by seeking to please with every colour while denying any inner substance. He who is led aside by triviality has to pay for it in his nobler nature; but he who deliberately seeks triviality is—well, happy, I suppose, because he has nothing to atone for!

"You see how talkative you have made me! But don't let me forget the main thing, which is that I should thank you once more. Good-bye and let me hear from you again soon, Your

"RICHARD WAGNER."

[1] Quoted in full by Hanslick in his *Musikalische Stationen*, and appearing also in the English translation of Wagner's letters.

Hanslick tells us that he had dared to hail "Tannhäuser" as the most significant production in grand opera since "Les Huguenots," "a statement which to-day (about 1880) still seems to me no mean compliment." And even at a later date one may sympathize with the views expressed by Wagner about Meyerbeer without finding a great deal in "Tannhäuser" to lift it above similar criticism.[1]

I do not intend here, or elsewhere in this study of Hanslick, to enter into any detailed survey of the Wagner-Hanslick territory. After all, it is mainly to Wagner and his disciples and biographers that we owe the incomplete and one-sided view of Hanslick that is current. Everyone who has so much as heard the name Hanslick immediately thinks of him in relation to Wagner. There may be an accompanying recollection that he was a strong supporter of Brahms, but that is often regarded as only a natural characteristic of an anti-Wagnerite. Wagner's own arrogant attitude towards Hanslick in *Mein Leben* is well known, but those who have read Hanslick's account of the reading of the "Meistersinger" libretto can hardly fail to regard Wagner's actions and his account of them as in the worst possible taste. Although the

[1] In 1891, on the occasion of the Meyerbeer centenary, Hanslick wrote an article in which he comments on Wagner's attitude to Meyerbeer. It appears in *Aus dem Tagebuch eines Musikers.*

"Meistersinger" incident took place some fifteen years later than the "Tannhäuser" correspondence, it will be convenient to give some account of it at this point, as Hanslick's attitude to Wagner remained substantially the same throughout his career.

First let us look at Wagner's version of the "Meistersinger" reading: "A curious incident occurred at the very beginning of my visit (to Vienna). I had to read the 'Meistersinger' aloud to the Standhartner family, as I had done everywhere else. As Dr. Hanslick was now supposed to be well disposed towards me, it was considered the right thing to invite him too. We noticed that as the reading proceeded the dangerous critic became more and more pale and depressed, and it was remarked by everyone that it was impossible to persuade him to stay on at the close, but that he took his leave there and then in an unmistakably vexed manner. My friends all agreed in thinking that Hanslick looked on the whole libretto as a lampoon aimed at himself, and had felt an invitation to the reading to be an insult." The pseudo-naivety of Wagner's attitude in writing the above has been remarked on by Mr. Ernest Newman, and even if we did not know that Beckmesser was named Hans Lich in the first sketch of the libretto we could hardly give Wagner credit for much subtlety or benevolence.

Hanslick gives his account of the incident as

follows: [1] "After the smothering heat of the 'Nibelungen' . . . 'Die Meistersinger,' a three-act opera whose text we had read out to us by Wagner himself at the house of one of the most amiable art-lovers in Vienna. In spite of details to which one must object (the diction, for example, is atrocious), the work as a whole remains a pleasing picture of German town life, sometimes bright, sometimes touching, based on simple relationships and enlivened by the joys and sufferings of simple people. Wagner will undoubtedly do a greater service to the German theatre with the easily grasped and easily staged 'Meistersinger' than with the 'Nibelungen': while the latter waits for a visionary future, the former is awaited by an opera-starved present. Wagner has opened up simultaneously two ways for himself. It cannot be a matter of indifference for German art which of the two he will choose in the future; whether he will prefer to be a Meistersinger or a Nibelung of his nation." This passage Hanslick thinks it worth while to reprint in his autobiography, but he says nothing further about the reading beyond a remark he made to Wagner about being unable to understand how he could write music to the list of "Weisen," which David enumerates in the first act, Wagner's reply being, "O, that flows past so easily in song that it doesn't offend."

There is a detailed criticism of "Die Meistersinger"

[1] *Aus dem Concertsaal*, p. 254.

in the first volume of Hanslick's *Die Moderne Oper*. Its general trend is adverse. While he finds the subject admirable and even some of the situations in the work well devised, its great length and over-elaboration of prosaic details all but kills it, and he comes to the conclusion that what it suffers from most is Wagner's lack of any sense of humour. The criticism as a whole has much to recommend it[1] even if one can hardly understand Hanslick's failure to see anything in the overture which he condemns as "a piece of music of painful artificiality and absolutely brutal effect." However, amid much that makes the reader smile, mostly at Wagner's, not at Hanslick's, expense—it is surely fatal for a musician to take Wagner too seriously!—there are some remarks I should like to quote if only to show that Hanslick's general condemnation does not blind him to the beauty of certain passages. Quite early in his criticism he says, "The beauties of the work are as little to be denied as its weak and repellent pages; it contains scenes that are amongst Wagner's happiest musical inspirations, and then again wearisome long passages of boring or disagreeable music." A little later we read, "Pogner's address comes like a ray of sunlight in the boring

---

[1] In *Aus meinem Leben* (Vol. 2, p. 177) Hanslick, writing some twenty years later, confesses that he thinks much better of the "Meistersinger" as a whole, but says that he retracts not a word of what he had written about the other operas.

thick musical mist of what precedes it. The uniformly fine feeling which invests this piece, with its melodious and beautifully harmonized principal motive, make it one of the highlights of the opera." Of the finale of the second act Hanslick says, "It was a very good idea of Wagner's not to end the act with the crowded street spectacle, but rather to let the people gradually go off and the noise die down. We see the night-watchman alone walking slowly through the empty moonlit streets—one of those poetic-picturesque effects which Wagner understands better than any." Walther's prize song is warmly praised, especially for not losing itself in Wagner's usual "endlessness" after the third bar. But Hanslick thinks that its many verses and later repetitions spoil its effect. The Quintet receives unqualified approval, part of which is attributed to the fact that it comes "after three hours of declamatory solo-singing over the waves of 'endless melody' or chorus din." Adverse criticism is summed up in the statement that "in the 'Meistersinger' the voice as such is not only something incomplete, it is simply nothing at all. The accompaniment is everything; it is an independent symphonic creation, an orchestral fantasia with accompanying voices *ad libitum*." This, to Hanslick's mind, and many of us can agree with him to a greater or less extent, is a reversal of the natural order of things. He says, "If you were to give a skilled Wagner-musician nothing but the text and the orchestral accompaniment of the opera he would be able to fit a passable vocal part to it extempore. . . . But given the voice part alone no one would succeed in restoring the lost orchestral parts." It will be seen that the symphonic nature of the music did not escape Hanslick's notice, although it has not always been grasped by "Leit Motiv"-deafened Wagnerites, and the criticism of the "sprechgesang" is not an unreasonable one. It may be a restricted view which insists that a grateful vocal part is of paramount importance in opera and that "an orchestral fantasia with vocal accompaniment" is not a solution to the operatic problems of time and continuity, but it can at least be logically defended and a mass of the finest music of all periods can be produced as examples of achievement not incompatible with such a viewpoint. There can be little doubt that Hanslick was in the main right about Wagner and his music dramas. To make such a statement is not to belittle Wagner's tremendous achievement, but it was an achievement which constituted a gigantic and conclusive proof that no completely satisfying solution of the operatic problem is to be found along those lines. It is about as certain as anything can be that the nearest approach to a completely satisfying result lies in quite the opposite direction—in the direction, that is, of formalism or, as some would no doubt prefer to call it, artificiality. A true union of music and drama is probably past praying for: all that can be expected is that they should occasionally be peaceful and happy neighbours. But here I am afraid Hanslick, much as he disagreed with Wagner, would not have agreed with me. Throughout his criticism Hanslick tended to a belief, as can be seen in the short passage about the "Meistersinger" quoted above, in the power of opera to portray essentially human situations and emotions. It was that belief which partly blinded him to the beauty of Gluck's operas—a much more serious defect, to my mind, than any lack of appreciation of Wagner. Ambros was a Gluck enthusiast, but much though Hanslick esteemed Ambros, he could not bring himself to sympathize wholeheartedly with him in this matter. He found the other-worldly atmosphere of Gluck's operas too oppressive and their formal classicism too cold for his liking. Here again, though we may disagree, we cannot but admire the sincerity with which his views are expressed. Richard Specht in his book on Brahms gives one of the most detailed first-hand accounts of Hanslick that we have. I shall have occasion to consider it later, but meantime there is a sentence in it which is appropriate to the present considerations. He says, "What seems incontrovertible is that he (Hanslick) was far more honest than people believed, and that even his attacks on Wagner were not due to rancour of any sort, but rather to some inner insufficiency; and his condemnation by those who are wise after the event is not without a certain cheapness."[1] This from one who was in a favourable position to judge, but who was not, as will be seen later, by any means prejudiced in Hanslick's favour, should add emphasis to the evidence of Hanslick's own writing about Wagner's work. He spared himself no trouble to become thoroughly acquainted with the early operas, with the "Ring" (there are long detailed accounts of the Bayreuth performances and of the preposterous "literature" which they called forth), "Tristan" and "Meistersinger." Whenever he sees a feature to admire, and it happens not infrequently, he is eloquent in his admiration and praise, but he can never forget that, magnificent as much of the achievement of Wagner is, it is, alas, directed to fatally wrong ends. And who, we may ask, has turned out to be right in the long run? Consider the following passage written after visiting Bayreuth.

"It is unthinkable that this method will, as Wagner holds, be the only valid opera style from now on, in short 'the Art of the Future.' When an art has arrived at a period of the greatest luxury it is then in decline, not ascending. Wagner's opera style exists in an atmosphere of superlatives; but no superlative has a future, it is the end, not the beginning. Richard

[1] Richard Specht, *Johannes Brahms*, trans. Blom, p. 173.

Wagner from 'Lohengrin' onwards has laid down a new way for himself which is vitally dangerous; but it is a way for him alone; whoever follows will perish and the public will witness this misfortune with indifference."[1] The shade of Hanslick may, I think, be allowed a quiet smile of satisfaction at the accuracy of his forecast.

As I have already pointed out, there is no mention by Hanslick in his account of the "Meistersinger" reading of any knowledge he may have had of Wagner's original name for Beckmesser. Although it is more than likely that all the facts were well known to him, he nowhere credits Wagner himself with the origin of the association Hanslick-Beckmesser but, towards the end of *Aus meinem Leben*, refers to it as the work of the "Wagnerites." With exquisite irony he suggests that these Wagnerites only show that they do not understand their own master. "The town-clerk Beckmesser," he says, "is a typical pedant concerned with trifles and matters of secondary importance; a Philistine without any sense of beauty and without any spiritual horizon, a narrow-minded petty critic who chalks down every false accentuation, every note departing from the 'rules,' as a crime against art, and believes he has annihilated the singer when he has added up these single faults. I have never tackled Wagner on trifles, never tracked

[1] *Musikalische Stationen*, p. 247.

down particular breaches of rules in his works—my criticisms of the past forty years are adequate proof that such pedantry does not concern me. It is quite foreign to my nature to approach a significant phenomenon with a foot-rule of formal correctness and pick out orthographic and grammatic shortcomings. I have always allowed only big issues, only fundamental considerations, to weigh against Wagner's music-dramas. What I have reproached him with is the violation of music by words, the unnaturalness and exaggeration of the expression, the annihilation of the singer and of the art of singing by unvocal writing and orchestral din, the displacement of the melody of song by declamatory recitation, ennervating monotony and measureless expansion, and finally, the unnatural, stilted progression of his diction, a diction which offends every feeling for fine speech. When I mentioned details it was mostly in a favourable, not in an unfavourable, way. Such criticism is, it seems to me, anything but Beckmesserish."

Yet it may be supposed that such a formidable indictment would still appear "Beckmesserish" to Wagner and his followers, particularly the followers. Hanslick's point of view was just fundamentally opposed to the theory and practice of Wagner, and it would be unprofitable, except for any who may at this time of day still be unfamiliar with the nature of such opposition, to explore in detail the mass of his Wagner criticism. No one curious enough to read an essay on Hanslick is likely to be unfamiliar with anti-Wagner criticism. Hanslick was as eloquent against, as Bernard Shaw some years later was for, Wagner. As a matter of fact, Shaw's last two pieces of music criticism were written about Bayreuth performances in 1894, the year in which Hanslick published his *Aus meinem Leben*. It is amusing to find the perfect Wagnerite writing, "The opening performance of Parsifal this season was, from the purely musical point of view, as far as the principal singers were concerned, simply an abomination. The bass howled, the tenor bawled, the baritone sang flat, and the soprano, when she condescended to sing at all, and did not merely shout her words, screamed, except in the one un-screamable song of Herzeleide's death, in which she subsided into commonplaceness." No doubt Hanslick would have agreed heartily, laying the blame, how-ever, not on the singers alone, as Shaw did, but further back on Wagner himself. Writing in 1935, Shaw, in his preface to *London Music in* 1888–89, says, "The wars of religion were not more blood-thirsty than the discussions of the Wagnerites and the Anti-Wagnerites. I was, of course, a violent Wagnerite; and I had the advantage of knowing the music to which Wagner grew up, whereas many of the most fanatical Wagnerites . . . knew no other music than Wagner's, and believed that the music of Donizetti and Meyerbeer had no dramatic quality whatever." And in a later paragraph, "Though I used to scarify the fools who said that Wagner's music was formless, I should not now think the worse of Wagner if, like Bach and Mozart, he had combined the most poignant dramatic expression with the most elaborate decorative design. It was necessary for him to smash the superstition that this was obligatory; to free dramatic melody from the tyranny of arabesques; and to give the orchestra symphonic work instead of rosalias and rum-tum; but now that this and all the other musical superstitions are in the dustbin, and the post-Wagnerian harmonic and contrapuntal anarchy is so complete that it is easier technically to compose another Parsifal than another Bach's Mass in B Minor or Don Giovanni, I am no longer a combatant anarchist in music, not to mention that I have learnt that a successful revolution's first task is to shoot all revolutionists." Even although there may be a visible strain in making these two extremes meet, they will perhaps hold together until I move safely out of Wagner territory.[1]

[1] When I visited Wagner's lake-side home at Triebschen, Lucerne, in 1969, I was amused and rather gratified to see on the bookshelves in one of his rooms several volumes of Hanslick's works.

CHAPTER III

"THE BEAUTIFUL IN MUSIC"

AS a result of occasional articles for the *Sonntags-blätter*, Hanslick was invited to become music critic for the *Wiener Zeitung* in 1848, and he wrote for this paper until 1850, when official duties connected with the Ministry of Finance required him to sever his connection with Vienna and take up uncongenial duties in Klagenfurt for two years. It is characteristic of Hanslick that he could never decide to give up the office work he disliked so much and take a chance with full-time music journalism or teaching. He frankly admits that he found it impossible to give up a sure position, however small it might be, for a precarious musical career. It was only after thirteen years of official duties in various Government offices that he found himself, on being offered a professorship at the University of Vienna, at last in a position to say good-bye to affairs of State. It had always been Hanslick's ideal, as he himself rather naively tells us, to be a professor. By that, of course, he meant the occupant of a university chair and not merely one of those teachers of singing or pianoforte who so often usurp the dignified title! The mantle did not fall upon him, however, until 1861, although he was able to prepare himself for it by giving lectures as

"Privatdozent" from 1856, that is, two years after the publication of his famous book, *Vom Musikalisch-Schönen.*

It will be seen, then, that this in many ways remarkable treatise was a comparatively early production written while its author was only twenty-nine and not yet in a position to devote his whole time to music. Much of the criticism it called forth and still calls forth has been based on the assumption that it represents Hanslick's mature and final views on the problems of musical æsthetics. While the work demands far more attention than many superficial critics have given it, it must not be taken to represent Hanslick's idea of a complete æsthetic. In later years Hanslick had the best of reasons for not expanding the book; he was no longer sufficiently interested in the problems it raises. He felt, he tells us, that more was to be gained by a study of the history of his art than by a consideration of the abstruse æsthetic problems into which any further development of his original treatise would inevitably lead him. He realized that there is no end to theorizing about the ultimate nature of music or "the Beautiful" in music. "Various epochs, various nations, various schools, have answered the question, 'What is beautiful in music?' in quite different ways. The more I studied the history of music the more vaporous and vague did musical æsthetics appear to be—almost like a mirage." A few sentences in *Aus meinem Leben*,[1] however, are very important in relation to the treatise and must be given here as exactly as translation will allow.

"The nature of music is more difficult to put into philosophical categories than the nature of painting because the vital concepts of 'Form' and 'Content' not only are not constant but refuse to be separated. If one claims that purely instrumental music has a definite meaning (in vocal music it is furnished by the poem and not by the music), then one must throw overboard the most precious pearls of the art of sound, as no one can possibly prove or even 'fill in' a meaning as apart from the form. On the other hand, I quite agree that it is misleading to speak, as I did in my book, in a way which brought me most opposition, simply of the 'meaninglessness' of instrumental music. How can significant form be distinguished scientifically from empty form in music?"

Those who are acquainted with the art criticism of Clive Bell and Roger Fry will realize that I have allowed myself to translate Hanslick's "beseelte Form" by an expression invented by Mr. Bell somewhere about 1914. The concept of "significant form" is indeed the basis of much of Mr. Bell's illuminating criticism, and although Roger Fry did not go all the way with Mr. Bell in the importance he attaches to "significant form," he realizes its great importance in

[1] P. 243.

any attempt to arrive at æsthetic values. In the last chapter of *Vision and Design* there is a paragraph which sums up at its very least the value of Mr. Bell's theory. It runs as follows: "With regard to the expression of emotion in works of art, I think that Mr. Bell's sharp challenge to the usually accepted view of art as expressing the emotions of life has been of great value. It has led to an attempt to isolate the purely æsthetic feeling from the whole complex of feelings which may, and generally do, accompany the æsthetic feeling when we contemplate a work of art." If for "Mr. Bell's sharp challenge" we substitute in the above "Hanslick's sharp challenge," I think we have a statement which should be equally valid. I say "should be," because unfortunately music criticism has in the majority of cases failed to learn anything from Hanslick's pioneer work, even although it was presented with the idea of "significant form" translated into practically every European language some thirty years before the publication of Clive Bell's *Art*. The only conclusion one can come to is that people either have never read *Vom Musikalisch-Schönen* or else have completely failed to understand it. Instead of calling forth a statement like the following, "It seems to me that this attempt to isolate the elusive element of the pure æsthetic reaction from the compounds in which it occurs has been the most important advance of modern times in practical æsthetic,"[1] as it might well have done, Hanslick's work has been met with such manifestly absurd comments as, "In spite of a Hanslick, for whom music was only an arabesque-like play of tones, or a kaleidoscope, it still produces its psychological effects, and the recognition of this should be the chief end of all musical instruction."[2] Hanslick and his works have survived mainly as a butt for criticism by Wagnerites, and indeed Mr. Newman, in his latest volumes on Wagner, goes the length of declaring that it is as well for Hanslick that he did not become a supporter of Wagner, as then he would have lost the negative fame he earned as his opponent. If only for *Vom Musikalisch-Schönen* itself, Hanslick has no need of *negative* fame.

I do not propose to deal in any great detail with the treatise here. It is available in German (in which it ran to nine editions), English,[3] French, Italian and Russian, and cannot fail to make its meaning abundantly clear if carefully read. In the preface to the seventh edition (from which the existing English version was made) Hanslick puts his case quite shortly. "I am quite at one with those who hold that the ultimate worth of the beautiful must ever depend upon the immediate verdict of the feelings. But at

[1] Roger Fry, *Vision and Design*, p. 300 (Phœnix Library).
[2] Karl Nef, *An Outline of the History of Music* (Eng. trans., Columbia Univ. Press, p. 10).
[3] *The Beautiful in Music* (Novello, 1891).	Liberal Arts Press, 1957.

the same time I firmly adhere to the conviction, that all the customary appeals to our emotional faculty can never show the way to a single musical law." He then states what he calls the *negativ Hauptsatz* of the enquiry "which is mainly and primarily directed against the widely accepted doctrine that the office of music is 'to represent feelings.'" . . . This is balanced by the positive proposition that "the beauty of a composition is specifically musical—*i.e.*, it inheres in the combinations of musical sounds and is independent of all alien, extra-musical notions." It is hardly surprising if in the age of the Wagner music-drama and the Liszt symphonic poems Hanslick found himself having to insist more on what music is *not* than on what it actually is. In the welter of programme music and monstrous quasi-literary efforts of Wagner and his disciples the case for the opposition had to be driven home as emphatically as possible, and it was only natural that the negative aspect should also be pounced upon by Hanslick's critics almost as if the positive side did not exist. But now that the lapse of time enables us to see the nineteenth century in its true musical proportions, surely the "attempt to isolate the elusive element of the pure æsthetic reaction from the compounds in which it occurs" can be properly appreciated as one of great importance in the study of musical values.

In his book on Berlioz, Mr. W. J. Turner has made a statement which represents probably the most unqualified expression to be met with in contemporary music criticism of the views originally put forth by Hanslick. "I am of the opinion," says Mr. Turner, "that the whole ancient controversy about programme music was the result of a misconception and is a controversy about an illusion. The text of an opera, the words of a song, the programme of a symphony or tone poem or whatever name in the future may be given to any musical composition is of no importance or significance whatever. I know this will be going too far for the majority of musicians, nevertheless I am convinced that it is true, literally and strictly true." It was just this truth on which Hanslick was one of the first, if not *the* first, to insist. It would take up space out of proportion to my present purpose were I to enter on the well-beaten track of the discussion of programme music, but one of the simplest and most fundamental aspects of the matter is worthy of short consideration here—"the words of a song." In a passage I have already quoted Hanslick says simply that in vocal music the definite meaning is furnished by the poem and not by the music. Considerable space is given to this view in *Vom Musikalisch-Schönen*, where Hanslick takes a definite and very well-known example to illustrate his meaning, Gluck's "Che farò." It is a passage which may still prove a stumbling block to a modern reader because, as Hanslick says, this aria has been hailed by several generations "as most aptly conveying the supreme grief which the *words* express." He points out that one Boyé, a contemporary of Gluck, had observed that "precisely the same melody would accord equally well, if not better, with words conveying exactly the reverse" (in much the same irrefutable way, surely, as Sir James Jeans has pointed out in our own day that there is nothing in pianoforte "touch" but what is imagined by the player or listener). It may be accounted dreadful heresy nowadays to agree with the all but unknown Boyé, but is the balance of the evidence not, after all, in his favour? It may be difficult for us to dissociate the melody from the meaning contained in the text, but once the effort is made, the conventional idea of the major mode, a speeding up of tempo and a slight perkiness of utterance will complete the transition to another world. As against that we have Sir Donald Tovey's statement [1] that "in 'Che farò' and the echo songs in the first act of 'Orféo' Gluck's highest pathos is expressed in the major mode. . . . The study of Gluck's most serious melody is a useful method of shaking modern criticism out of its conventional values." Now it may be an indisputable fact that Gluck does so use the major mode, but does it prove

[1] Essay on Gluck in *The Heritage of Music* (O.U.P.).

anything about music? The middle sections of the
funeral marches of Beethoven and Chopin are also
very pathetic, but only, it may well be argued, by
contrast with the surrounding conventional minor
gloom. All the ordinary emotional meaning of music
is derived from sequences of sounds whose three
prime factors are pitch, quality and intensity. The
effects of tempo are more or less general and, in
European music for the past two centuries at least,
the conventional idea of major and minor is respectively as happy and sad, to put it at its simplest.[1]

One further illustration may perhaps be presented
in substantiation of this view. The first movement of
Mozart's G minor symphony is usually regarded as
expressive of melancholy if not of positive tragedy.

----

[1] In *Vom Musikalisch-Schönen* Hanslick puts it thus
(Eng. trans., p. 37): "What part of the feelings, then, can music
represent, if not the subject involved in them? Only the *dynamic*
properties. It may reproduce the motion accompanying psy-
chical action according to its momentum: speed, slowness,
strength, weakness, increasing and decreasing intensity. But
motion is only one of the concomitants of feeling, not the
feeling itself."

In case major and minor as "respectively happy and sad"
may seem an oversimplification, I would point out that this
view does not rule out the possibility of the major mode
having a greater capacity for the expression of pathos than the
minor. On the contrary, it establishes that possibility in view
of ordinary human experience. Grief at the death of a friend
touches breaking point, not so much at the sense of bereave-
ment itself as at the recollection of happiness shared. Gluck,
we may assume, knew this and translated it literally into music.

Rossini's overture to "The Barber," on the other hand, is regarded as light and sparkling. In his analysis of the G minor symphony Sir Donald Tovey says [1] "we need not be shocked to find that the language of the opening of the G minor symphony is much the same as that of the Overture." His contention is, if I may put it together very sketchily by quoting three of his own sentences, (1) "The Symphony in G Minor has been compared with all manner of tragedies. . . ." (2) "If we are to understand Mozart we must rid our minds of the presumption that a tragic issue is intrinsically greater than any other. . . ." (3) "Mozart's whole language is, and remains throughout, the language of comic opera." Now the difficulty I have with the trend of this argument is that it seems to require the removal of Mozart's Symphony to the supposedly very much lower level of Rossini's Overture, whereas I am inclined to exalt the Overture to the extent to which I find it echoed in Mozart's Symphony. This may simply be a different way of looking at the same thing, but I confess I am somewhat disturbed when Tovey says Rossini's Overture fits "The Barber" admirably, because long before I knew that the Overture was written, as Tovey reminds us, for another opera, I felt at a loss to account for what I took to be its serious and somewhat tragic nature in association

[1] *Essays in Musical Analysis*, Vol 1, p. 193.

with the tomfoolery of " The Barber." On learning
that it was originally written for an *opera seria*,
"Aureliana in Palmira," and did service to another
opera, "Elisabetta, Regina d'Inghilterra," before re-
placing an overture, now lost, which Rossini originally wrote for "The Barber," I felt my instinctive
reaction to the piece had found its justification.
Tovey, however, talks of its "feebly shrill and
bickering opening," and declares that "even to those
of us who are most fond of the *Barbiere*, this sort of
thing hardly bears mentioning in relation to the
G minor Symphony. The language, we admit, is
common to both: where does the gulf lie?" I contend
that to the extent to which the language of these two
works is similar, there is no gulf, only a difference in
degree. The Overture does not prove the lack of
tragedy in the Symphony, but the tragedy of the
Symphony by normal conventions can be held as
proving the presence of tragedy in the Overture,
that is, assuming proof in such matters to be possible
which, in fact, it is not. But there is an illuminating
passage in Stendhal's *Vie de Rossini* which is particularly important as showing a contemporary point
of view. Speaking of this very overture he says,
"Elle se trouve ainsi avoir à exprimer les combats de
l'amour at de l'orgeuil dans une des âmes les plus
hautes dont l'histoire ait gardé la mémoire, et les
folies du barbier Figaro. Le plus petit changement

de temps suffit souvent pour donner l'accent de la plus profonde mélancolie à l'air le plus gai. Essayez de chanter en ralentissant le mouvement, l'air de Mozart: *Non più andrai farfallone amoroso.*"

In much the same way Hanslick adduces the examples of Gluck's borrowing freely in his serious works from his earlier comic operas and also the now well-known case of Bach's Christmas Oratorio. Dr. Albert Schweitzer, great champion of the pictorial aspect of Bach's music, has said," We must neither overestimate nor underestimate the bearing of this fact [the wholesale borrowings from secular cantatas] on the artistic value of the Christmas Oratorio. Spitta underrates it, saying that the fact that the music was originally written for another text does not deprive it of any of its beauty. Others hold that the discovery of the *provenance* of the choruses and arias dissipates a good deal of the charm of the work." [1] Even Dr. Schweitzer cannot find anything to justify Bach's procedure in this matter. "It is almost incredible," he says, "that the same artist who insisted so strongly on characteristic expression in music could at another time constrain his music so barbarously to fit an alien text." [2] Hanslick's conclusion is that it is obvious that "vocal

---

[1] *J. S. Bach*, by Albert Schweitzer (trans. Newman), Vol. 2, p. 304.

[2] *Ibid.*, p. 283.

music, the theory of which can never determine the nature of music generally, is likewise in practice not in a position to give the lie to principles derived from the conception of instrumental music." [1] It is interesting to find Dr. Schweitzer, as we might expect, flatly contradicting Hanslick in an earlier part of his book. He quotes the following passage from *Vom Musikalisch-Schönen:* "It is æsthetically a matter of indifference if Beethoven worked upon definite subjects in every one of his compositions; we do not know these subjects; therefore, so far as the work is concerned, they do not exist. It is the work alone which lies before us, without any commentary; and just as the jurist ignores everything that is not embodied in acts and deeds, so nothing exists for the æsthetic judgment that lies outside the work of art." Schweitzer maintains that the music is only "the hieroglyph, in which are recorded the emotional qualities of the visions of the concrete imagination."

At the risk of seeming to overload this part of my essay with quotations, I must lift one or two more sentences from Sir Donald Tovey's writings. In the opening of his analysis of Beethoven's "Pastoral" Symphony he says, "The first and the last word of

---

[1] My translation here differs from the published English version, in which the point of this difficult sentence seems rather to be missed. (P. 84, 1891 edition; p 60, 1957 reprint).

common sense about programme music in general was said by Beethoven on this symphony in particular. He said it was 'the expression of feelings rather than painting.' " A later passage in the same analysis must now be quoted in full:

"In the whole symphony there is not a note of which the musical value would be altered if cuckoos and nightingales, and country folk, and thunder and lightning, and the howling and whistling of the wind, were things that had never been named by man, either in connexion with music or with anything else. Whether we have words for common objects and events of the countryside, or whether we have no words, there are feelings evoked by these objects in proportion to our intelligent susceptibility; and the great master of any language, whether that language be music, painting, sculpture, architecture, or speech, can invoke the deepest part of these feelings in his own terms. And his art will always remain pure as long as he holds to Beethoven's dictum; which may be philosophically retranslated 'more the expression of feelings than the illustration of things.' "

The particular sentence in that passage to which I wish to draw attention is, "the great master . . . can invoke the deepest part of these feelings in his own terms." If by "the deepest part" we mean, as far as music is concerned, that part of the feelings capable of being expressed in terms of motion ("motion in the wider sense, of course, according to which the increasing and decreasing force of a single note or chord is 'motion' also"[1]), Hanslick would have agreed with Tovey up to that point, but would still have protested that Beethoven's "mehr Ausdruck der Empfindung als Malerei," whether literally or "philosophically translated," was no more likely to ensure the purity of the art of music than the invention of a theme or the writing down of several "symbolic" sounds can ensure the completion of a musical composition. "With special reference to the creative action of the composer," he says, "we should bear in mind that it always consists in the grouping and fashioning of musical elements. The sovereignty of the emotions, so falsely reputed to be the main factor in music, is nowhere more completely out of place than when it is supposed to govern the musician in the act of composing, and when the latter is regarded as a kind of inspired improvisation."[2] Along with this we may place Tovey's statement, "In a voluminous composition there is naturally an immense amount of laborious work, such as the scoring of *tuttis*, which common sense forbids the composer to tackle while the flow of the composition needs his attention. The state of inspiration can nevertheless be maintained throughout these more mechanical tasks

---

[1] Hanslick, *Vom Musikalisch-Schönen*, Eng. trans., p. 38. (Reprint p. 24).

[2] *Ibid.*, p. 100. (Reprint p. 72).

if they are undertaken while waiting for light on other problems, or deferred until the rest of the work has been digested." [1] The phrase "needs his attention" and the word "problems" indicate that mental and not merely emotional activity is required in much less mechanical work even than "the scoring of *tuttis.*" In fact, as Hanslick says, the whole process of musical creation is one which "requires quiet and subtle thought, such as none who have not actually essayed it can comprehend." Though feeling is no doubt the original motive power and though musical development will be carried out in a manner which is not out of keeping with the original feeling, the act of composition can never be one continuous flow of primary emotion. "Expression of feelings" must surely therefore be regarded as at least an inadequate if not completely misleading definition of the function of music, or, for that matter, of any art. In his book *The Meaning of Art*, Mr. Herbert Read, after some consideration of Tolstoy's definition of art as "transmitting" feeling, suggests an amendment as follows: "I would say that the function of art is not to transmit *feeling* so that others may experience the same *feeling*. That is only the function of the crudest forms of art —'programme music,' melodrama, sentimental fiction and the like. The real function of art is to express *feeling* and transmit *understanding*." The important

---

[1] *Musical Matter and Form*, p. 27.

point to note, however, is that the feeling or emotion expressed by the artist is *not* the emotion experienced by the spectator or listener. The composer's art is the ordering of inspiration, having its origin in emotion, into a form which arouses a responsive emotion in the listener. But this responsive emotion, as Mr. Read points out, is "an emotion totally different in kind from the emotion experienced and expressed by the artist in the act of creating the work of art. It is better described as a state of wonder or admiration, or more coldly but more exactly as a state of recognition."[1]

This fact is one which is much more liable to be lost sight of in music than in any of the other arts, because the material of music has of itself an emotional effect quite apart from the art form in which it is presented to us as a composition. This is dealt with also by Hanslick. He says, "The power which music possesses of profoundly affecting the nervous system cannot be ascribed so much to the *artistic* forms created by and appealing to the mind, as to the *material* with which music works and which Nature has endowed with certain inscrutable affinities of a physiological order." And again, "the more over-powering the effect is in a physical—*i.e.*, in a pathological sense, the less is it due to *æsthetic* causes. Another element must therefore be considered in the production and reception of music, an element which

[1] Much the same point has been made more recently by Ernest Ansermet in his book *Les Fondemonts de la musique dans la conscience humaine* and his LP record "What Everyone Should Know about Music."

represents the pure (unvermischt) æsthetic of this art, and, in contrast to the specifically musical stirring of the feelings, approximates to the general prerequisites of beauty in all the other arts. This is the act of pure perception" (reine Anschauung).[1] Here we are as near as can be to Mr. Read's "state of recognition."

The fifth chapter of Hanslick's treatise is devoted to the consideration of æsthetic hearing as opposed to pathological hearing of music. One might even put it simply as the difference between hearing and listening. In case it should be thought that parallels with the other arts have been overstressed, it should be noticed that Hanslick clearly states that the mental activity of the true listener to music is "quite peculiar to music because musical works instead of being fixed and presented to the mind at once in their completeness, develop gradually and thus do not permit the listener to linger at any point, or to interrupt the train of thought." In this connection there is a very interesting passage in Roger Fry's *Essay in Æsthetics* [2] which suggests that this gradual development may not even be so peculiar to music as Hanslick thought and as we are still apt to think. "It seems probable," says Mr. Fry, "that our appre-

[1] *Vom Musikalisch-Schönen*, p. 150. This translation differs in some particulars from the published English version, p. 122, (Reprint p. 88).

[2] In *Vision and Design*.

ciation of unity in pictorial design is of two kinds. We are so accustomed to consider only the unity which results from the balance of a number of attractions presented to the eye simultaneously in a framed picture that we forget the possibility of other pictorial forms.

"In certain Chinese paintings the length is so great that we cannot take in the whole picture at once, nor are we intended to do so. Sometimes a landscape is painted upon a roll of silk so long that we can only look at it in successive segments. As we unroll it at one end and roll it up at the other we traverse wide stretches of country, tracing, perhaps, all the vicissitudes of a river from its source to the sea, and yet, when this is well done, we have received a very keen impression of pictorial unity.

"Such a successive unity is, of course, familiar to us in literature and music, and it plays its part in the graphic arts. It depends upon the forms being presented to us in such sequence that each successive element is felt to have a fundamental and harmonious relation with that which preceded it."

It is difficult to see how anyone reading Hanslick's treatise carefully can fail to come to the conclusion that it is not only, in the words of the writer of his obituary notice in the *Musical Times*, "a thoughtfully written and logically conceived treatise," but a work which in the major considerations of musical æsthetics holds good to-day just as it did over a hundred years ago when it was first written. The trouble is that as a result of superficial reading of it Hanslick has been credited with views which he never held or expressed. The writer of the obituary notice above referred to, for instance, goes on to say that "Hanslick maintains that the beauty of a musical composition lies in the music itself—the strains thereof *per se*—and that whatever charm it possesses is entirely free from extraneous or non-musical ideas." Now the first part of that sentence may stand, but that "whatever charm it possesses is entirely free from extraneous or non-musical ideas" Hanslick would have been the last to admit. To express his views properly the sentence would have to run, "whatever *musical value* it possesses *must be judged* entirely apart from extraneous or non-musical ideas"—which is a very different matter. No one was more conscious of the "charm" and emotional power of music itself, music in the raw, as it were, than Hanslick, but he held, and rightly held, that in a true æsthetic it was necessary to distinguish between this raw emotion and the actual perception or recognition of the beautiful in music. And is not that just the purport of the following passage? "Certainly a criticism or an admiration that scorns the musical phenomena does not thereby become poetical; on the contrary, the man who expects music to give him poetical ideas while he refuses to listen to it as music, will infallibly, if he looks at other things as he looks at music, value poetry for the information it conveys when paraphrased in prose, architecture for the problems it solves in engineering, science for its practical use, and in short, everything for its lower and more accidental qualities, and this is the very type and essence of the prosaic mind." Words written, be it noted, not by Hanslick but by Sir Donald Tovey! [1]

[1] *Essays in Musical Analysis*, Vol. 3, p. 5.

CHAPTER IV

HANSLICK'S MIND AND METHOD

THERE is a footnote to the later editions of *Vom Musikalisch-Schönen*[1] which has rather an interesting origin. Hanslick quotes it as from the first volume of *Die Moderne Oper*,[2] which is dated 1874, but it actually has its origin in a much earlier concert notice written for the *Presse* in 1860, only six years, that is, after the first publication of the treatise. In *Die Moderne Oper* the passage had been considerably rewritten to make it more in keeping with the title of the book, but some of the original sentences remain practically intact. The subject of the 1860 concert notice was a performance of two of Handel's oratorios, "Alexander's Feast" and "Israel in Egypt." Actual criticism of the work concludes with the sentence: "Of all great composers Handel is perhaps most the child of his age; he conforms to its taste in his operas nor does he belie it at all in his oratorios; the arias of the latter are quite like those of his operas. At performances of Handel's music, in which we meet antiquated mannerisms as well as effects of the greatest and most striking kind, we are reminded every now and again of the widely circulated axiom that the truly beautiful never loses its effect no matter how great the lapse of

[1] P. 106. English ed. p. 90 (Reprint p. 64).
[2] *Vorwort* p. vi.

time. For music this is little more than a pretty phrase." What follows at this point is somewhat different from the development of the same theme in *Die Moderne Oper*, but it is not sufficiently important to be translated here in detail. A few slightly altered sentences lead to an exact transcription of the last sentences as of the first. "It is not long since Adam Hiller of Leipzig declared that if ever Hasse's operas should fail to delight then general barbarism must ensue. Schubart, the Hohenasperg writer on musical æsthetics, said of Jomelli that it was unthinkable such a composer could ever be forgotten. And what are Hasse and Jomelli to us now?" The quotation ends here in *Vom Musikalisch-Schönen*, but the continuation in *Die Moderne Oper* differs from the original 1860 notice mainly again to suit its nature as an introduction to a book on opera. In both cases, however, the reader is referred to the history of music which shows, Hanslick says, that musical values are relative and not absolute. There is rather an amusing alteration in the last sentence of the original notice when it is transcribed for *Die Moderne Oper*. Originally it ran, "The history of music is also the truest mirror for the future. It teaches us that an average life of from 100 to 150 years testifies to the extremely strong constitution of a musical composition; in secular music such years are seldom reached even by the most celebrated works." In *Die Moderne Oper* this reads, "History teaches us that operas for whose immortality one would have wagered one's life, enjoy an average life of from forty to fifty years, a period outlived by only a few original works, but on the other hand hardly ever reached by the bulk of favourite light operas." The phrase which I have translated by "would have wagered one's life" occurs in the sentence preceding the one I have quoted above in the 1860 original, and is used in connection with the view that Haydn's symphonies were bound to live for ever. Now I set no great store by such detective work as these observations may appear to have involved on my part, but it seems that this elaborate patchwork method of writing was rather characteristic of Hanslick, and I think it is not without its significance for his work as a whole. It would appear that Hanslick was not the facile writer many have declared him to be, but rather one who, like Berlioz, wrote laboriously but gave the impression of quick spontaneity. I have come across a number of passages which have been made, sometimes with minor alterations, to do duty more than once, and although I am well aware that everyone who writes at all occasionally effects such economy in his output, these domestic borrowings are not usually apparent or quite of the nature of Hanslick's. There is a good example in the notice of one of Bach's cantatas, "Ich hatte viel Bekümmernis," which first appeared as a *Presse* contribution in 1863.[1] This cantata Hanslick regards as "indisputably one of the most beautiful and perhaps the most spirited of the long series of Bach's cantatas." After an account of the origin of the cantatas generally, Hanslick goes on to say, "The subject of this cantata is announced with the pregnant brevity of a thesis in the words of the first chorus 'Ich hatte viel Bekümmernis, aber deine Tröstungen erquicken meine Seele.' Out of this theme, introduced with the simplicity of a plain straightforward narrative, Bach develops an arresting spiritual painting, a sort of religious tragedy. The struggling of the distressed soul, now welling up in a storm of despair, now calmed to a death-like resignation, gradually subsides in the assurance of God's help and finally the troubled spirit rises in triumphant rapture. The cantata consists of a short orchestral introduction ('Sinfonia') and eight vocal numbers. Of the solos the finest undoubtedly is the first soprano aria in C minor with oboe obbligato. Bach knew how to turn its Pietist water into the truest wine of poesy. The aria has a sweetness, one might say youthfulness, of melody such as we seldom find in Bach. We should like to attribute part of the charm of this composition to its early date (1714), although the period of Bach's works is of little account as a rule. Of the two tenor arias the second, in F major, was

[1] *Aus dem Concertsaal*, p. 283.

omitted—not without justification; the first, in F minor, with its wonderfully harmonized ritornello (pointing prophetically to Schumann) is a real Bach masterpiece. The broadly-worked-out duet between soprano and bass—in some respects outmoded—makes a less favourable impression. The allegorical figure of the 'devout soul,' a well-known stereotyped phenomenon in the older protestant church music, appears here in direct conversation with the Saviour. Of the choruses one feels compelled to admire now one and now the other the longer one sinks oneself in them. If the opening chorus prepares with appropriate simplicity the proper foundation for the mood of the work, the subsequent chorus, 'Was betrübst du dich meine Seele,' builds up a gigantic edifice of rich polyphonic art inexhaustible in ever-new devices. Mendelssohn's setting of the same words is, in its gentle modernity, as a child compared with this." Thirty years later Hanslick again wrote about this cantata.[1] Several sentences are lifted from the earlier criticism and appear intact or with very little alteration in the later notice. The second tenor aria, in F major, is coupled with the first soprano aria in the sentence above referring to its "youthfulness." The reference to Schumann is omitted in connection with the other tenor aria and, instead, attention is drawn to the effectiveness of its accompanying recitative.

[1] *Aus dem Tagebuch eines Musikers*, p. 349.

The criticism of the duet is slightly extended, and then a passage is inserted giving evidence of support from Spitta for that criticism which, it appears, had met with decided opposition when first published. The actual nature of the criticism is of little importance nowadays, and we may disagree with it just as Schweitzer disagrees with Spitta and with Mattheson long before him. I draw attention to it only because of the light it throws on Hanslick's method of working. After the insertion about Spitta's views the criticism resumes, with only slight alterations, the course of that written thirty years earlier. It may seem strange that Hanslick should prefer to furbish up an old article rather than write a completely fresh one, and although the looking up of the old criticism could in this case be held to be due to the special circumstances in which Hanslick took advantage of the opportunity to justify an early opinion, there are other cases in which no other explanation can be given than that it seemed to him an unnecessary effort to write *de novo* on a subject on which he had already expressed his views clearly.[1] It is possible to interpret this as an attitude of mind similar to that expressed by Pilate's "What I have written, I have written," words which always have a certain fascination for a critic with convictions. But I think the likelier explanation is simply that Hanslick did not

[1] *Cf.* also pp. 71–72.

write easily or without careful deliberation.[1] It must be remembered that in those days it was not customary to serve up criticism like hot rolls on the morning after a concert. The introduction of this feature of musical journalism was one which Hanslick greatly deplored. His written criticism represented for the most part his carefully considered judgment of music and its performance, and it must often have seemed to him that in the discussion of the music as apart from the actual performance of it he could hardly do better than repeat, sometimes with greater or slightly altered emphasis, an earlier statement of his views. But this does not mean, as has been declared, that "he did not dream of revising a first impression." [2] As I have already pointed out,[3] even in the case of "Meistersinger" Hanslick modified his earlier views, and there are other cases, notably in connection with Berlioz's music, where he revised his judgment.[4] Everything indeed in Hanslick's writing points to

[1] This view is borne out by Hanslick's remarks about Ambros who, he says, could sit down and write at any hour of the day or night without the least preparation. "Other writers (including myself) require a quiet hour or so to collect their thoughts before they dip pen in ink—a sort of brooding. Ambros could have been suddenly awakened from sleep immediately either to continue the writing of his interrupted manuscript or begin a new chapter" (*Aus meinem Leben*, p. 236).

[2] Tovey, *Essays in Musical Analysis*, Vol. 2, p. 71.

[3] See footnote, p. 15.

[4] See also pp. 66–67 *re* his views on Mozart.

the fact that his reaction to music was a perfectly genuine one and that in his criticism he sought to analyse the various elements which contributed to his enjoyment or otherwise of the music presented to him. To some this may seem little enough to claim for the work of a music critic, but, after all, what more can be reasonably demanded? Attempts have been made to explain the function of the critic in various complicated and exalted terms. Criticism has been disembodied in the hope or belief that absolute and eternal values might be determined. But any proof of the existence of such absolute values remains yet to be given. The quality of music criticism as of any other art criticism depends on the experience, the cultural background, the general quality of mind of the critic, and it is only of value to us to the extent that *these* are known and esteemed by us. Hanslick had no illusions as to absolute musical values. He had insisted in *Vom Musikalisch-Schönen* on the isolation and recognition of the one isolable and basic feature of musical composition, the "specifically musical," and, having done so, showed at once the limits of absolute criticism and the necessarily subjective and relative nature of most musical judgment.

This leads us to the consideration of what has been regarded as a more serious charge against Hanslick, the limited range of his own musical appreciation. Richard Specht, who attended Hanslick's lectures, declares [1] that he showed more reverence than enthusiasm for the works of Bach and Handel and their predecessors, that it is doubtful whether he really appreciated Brahms's works to the full in spite of the admiration he often expressed for them, and that he was only truly at home in the superficial music of French opera or operetta. As against this, however, Specht has to admit Brahms's lasting friendship with Hanslick and the undoubted value he laid on his judgments. It is difficult indeed to see how the genuineness of Hanslick's attitude to Brahms can be doubted, and even if it was not so deeply under-standing as some may profess to have expected, it must be remembered that wisdom after the event is inclined to underestimate contemporary sympathy and insight.

With regard to Hanslick's attitude to sixteenth and seventeenth century music, there is a passage at the end of his *Aus meinem Leben* in which this is made absolutely clear. In the form of a conversation with his friend Theodor Billroth, Hanslick outlines his musical creed. He has been accused, he admits, of being a reactionary in music, but Billroth points out that what he (Hanslick) has written about Schumann, Brahms and Dvořák should be sufficient to dispose of that accusation. On the other hand, he has also been accused of a tendency to favour the work of his own time or that immediately preceding it at the

[1] Richard Specht, *Johannes Brahms* (Dent).

expense of the earlier and later classics. To this Hanslick replies that as far as Mozart and Beethoven are concerned it is inevitable that a critic's work should predispose him in favour of novelty. He would have to abstain altogether for some years from listening to the well-known symphonies, quartets and sonatas in order to come to them with the fresh enthusiasm of his early years. As regards music before the time of Mozart he says he must admit his sins "more penitently." He admits he belongs to his own age and "cannot help it if he would rather see all Heinrich Schütz's works burned than Brahms's German Requiem, rather the whole of Palestrina than Mendelssohn, rather all the concertos and sonatas of Bach than the quartets of Schumann and Brahms. For any one of 'Don Juan,' 'Fidelio' or 'Freischütz' he would sacrifice the whole of Gluck. A terrible confession, isn't it? But at least an honest one!" Hanslick goes on to point out that the foregoing statement is based only on the assumption that he is being compelled to choose between the alternatives of the old and new. All the same, he admits that about Bach, Handel and "the far more insufficient Gluck," he feels much the same as about Æschylus, Sophocles and Eurypides. "I marvel at them in humility but I cannot love them like Shakespeare, Schiller and Goethe. They are not flesh of our flesh, blood of our blood. Great, in their way, unapproachable artists they are, but they belong to a world of ideas long since exploded. The passage of time is in no art so speedy, so devastating, as in music. So it comes about that I only enjoy pre-Bach music for its historical interest; Bach, Handel and Gluck not exclusively but preponderantly with an artistic interest of a technical and historical nature. . . . From a historical point of view our living music begins for me with Bach and Handel. For my heart it begins only with Mozart and reaches its height in Beethoven, Schumann and Brahms." Along with these, however, there are, Hanslick insists, many composers of a lesser order whose work should not be disparaged. He instances Auber, Rossini, Meyerbeer, Spohr and Marschner and recalls the extent to which they can match living dramatic situations with appropriate music.

It is quite unjust to conclude from such remarks as these that Hanslick held the works of lesser composers in higher esteem than the music of the great masters. When he protested, as he did in connection with an essay by Ambros,[1] that uninspired attempts at serious music are more truly the "water weeds" of music than the talented frivolity to be found in Offenbach's operettas, when he deplores the time and trouble spent by Ambros in compiling the first volume of his history from musical sources so remote

[1] Ambros, *Bunte Blätter*, Vol. 2, *Die Musikalische Wasserpest*.

as hardly to be connected at all with music as we know it now,[1] he is not, as Mr. Newman's Max Morold would have it, showing that "his culture was of the slightest," or finding greater satisfaction, as Specht would suggest, in light music than in serious music, but simply emphasizing a fact which seems still to need emphasis in some quarters, that *historical enthusiasm is no real substitute for the direct æsthetic appeal of music*, and that a sprightly tune is infinitely to be preferred to dull pretentious symphonic labour.

It is obvious that for Hanslick the direct appeal of music was limited to work more or less of his own age. It was a limitation which he freely admitted, and because it is an admission which is much more rare on the part of a critic or historian than the profession of omniscience and omnidirectional responsiveness which we are so often left to assume, Hanslick's limitations have been denounced as if they, or others like them, were not common to all who respond genuinely to music of any particular period. Oscar Wilde truly said, "It is only an auctioneer who can equally and impartially admire all schools of art." [2] Hanslick's limitations are the limitations of a man in

---

[1] Hanslick's copy of Ambros's *History* has come into my possession and seems to indicate by his pencillings that he at least waded patiently through the first volume.

[2] In *The Critic as Artist*. There is a great deal in this brilliant essay of Wilde's which is clearly applicable to Hanslick's criticism.

whom a part of music at least awakens a genuine and immediate response. Better far to have such limitations and know them than to boast of a comprehensive view untouched by any emotion.

But it would be wrong to think that Hanslick overestimated the importance of his position or imagined his influence extended throughout the whole world of music. The last chapter of his autobiography is written in the form of a dialogue between himself and Billroth. In it Billroth asks the question, "Do you then, consider that your influence on artists is of no value at all?" And here is Hanslick's answer: "That influence is more than doubtful. I have always stood fast by the principle of speaking only to the public not to the artist. The critic who imagines he exerts an educative influence on artists, lives in pleasant self deception. As a rule the singer and the virtuoso regard as right only praise, never blame. In my long practice I can recollect extremely few cases where a suggestion of mine was actually regarded and my advice taken. And then it happened almost exclusively with our best artists—most often when I gave my opinion orally, perhaps at a final rehearsal. Printed criticism even in such cases was less willingly received. If my long activity as a critic has really been of any use, then it can only have been in its gradual educative influence on the public."

CHAPTER V

HIS CRITICISMS OF BACH AND HANDEL

IT would be no easy task to make a representative selection of Hanslick's writings from 1855 to 1864, when he was critic for the *Presse*, and from 1865 to the beginning of the present century, the period of his contributions to the *Neue Freie Presse*. It would certainly require a volume much larger than this has any intention of being and even then the difficulty would be in deciding what to leave out. For the present I must set myself very definite limits, and it seems to me I can hardly do better than allow them to be defined by Hanslick's own statement already cited, "From a historical point of view our living music begins for me with Bach and Handel. For my heart it begins only with Mozart and reaches its height in Beethoven, Schumann and Brahms." At the risk of laying greater emphasis on the works of these composers than Hanslick may have meant, I propose to take what seem to me to be representative passages from his books which will give the English reader some idea of the nature of his criticism. One or two passages referring to Bach and Handel have already been given. These may be supplemented by the following note on Bach's Third Brandenburg Concerto:

"A concerto by J. S. Bach for stringed instruments was exceedingly attractive. It is the third of six concertos published by Dehn in 1850, or rather the two outer movements of it as obviously a middle movement (probably a slow one in minor) has been lost.[1] An uncommonly strong, healthy, even if somewhat obstinate life pervades these close-knit themes which are presented to us without any inner contrast, without even the least interruption, yet richly developed. The chief charm lies, of course, in the lively and varied interplay of the parts. Through lack of contrasting wind instruments actual orchestral effects are to all intents and purposes lacking, yet the tossing of the theme from violins to violas and basses in the first movement is quite charming in its effect."[2]

And the following about the Orchestral Suite in D:

"Bach's characteristic and pleasing Suites are amongst the works of the old master which a modern public can assimilate with unconstrained enjoyment. A youthful, fresh spirit animates the forgotten concise forms; the contrapuntal art charms the knowing ear without confusing or tiring it; colourful contrast, such as that between the soft tenderness of the Airs and the amusing liveliness of the dance movements, heightens their effect. It is no wonder that the success

[1] Sir Donald Tovey recommends the insertion of a little-known *Adagio* for the "lost" movement. See his *Essays*, Vol. 2, p. 192. But perhaps the best solution is simply to omit the problematic cadential chords.

[2] *Aus dem Concertsaal*, p. 227.

of the D Suite at the Philharmonic Concert was complete. The original instrumentation was unaltered except for two clarinets added by Herr Dessoff because the high-pitched trumpet part in the original is difficult to perform nowadays." [1]

There is also an article on a performance of the "Christmas Oratorio" conducted by Brahms. Hanslick gives an account of Bach's borrowings from his other works in this composite work and concludes by pointing out:

"This example" (of turning old material to new account) "seems very suitable for making clearer two truths which are gladly ignored by the apologetic critics. Firstly, that musical expression, the 'psychological' capacity and development of music, was at a comparatively elementary stage in Bach's time seeing that love songs of Omphale and homage choruses to Saxon nobilities could simply be transplanted into religious works. Secondly, that in Bach the practical musician was after all not completely subdued by the strictly devoted Christian, but, on the contrary, the practical musician had no scruples about inserting secular pieces in the course of a religious work so long as the general character of these was suitable and he felt like rescuing a deserving piece of occasional music. Bach did not indulge in such borrowings or transcriptions so often or so inconsiderately as

[1] *Ibid.*, p. 229.

Handel; still, he did do so occasionally and in the Christmas Oratorio certainly in the grand manner." [1]

The above passage was written in 1864, but we find the same views more emphatically expressed in an article written in 1892 about another of Bach's cantatas, "Also hat Gott die Welt geliebt." He says this cantata "is outstanding in Bach's church music for its bright cheerful colouring. It suits the character of Whitsuntide for which it was intended—*intended*, even if not originally written for it. The two arias, to which Bach afterwards added an introductory and a fugal concluding chorus, applied not to the Deity ('dem lieben Gott') but to the Elector Christian of Weissenfels in Saxony. Bach composed in 1716, for a hunting banquet in honour of this gentleman, a mythological cantata as 'Tafelmusik.' He used it again later for several other festive occasions and finally transplanted two arias out of it, somewhat lengthened and enriched, into the church cantata 'Also hat Gott die Welt geliebt.' The well-known and delightful soprano aria 'Mein gläubiges Herzfrohlocke' ('My heart ever faithful') was originally that of the goddess of shepherds, Pales, and the bass aria 'Du bist geboren mir zu Gute' that of Pan, for the expression of secular sentiments. The change from happiest heathendom to Christian piety can hardly be detected. . . . This example proves two things.

[1] *Ibid.*, p. 306.

Firstly, the ambiguity of music; all melodies do not, it is true, fit any text, but there are many melodies which suit quite different and often quite hetero-geneous texts. Secondly, the falsity of the view that our classical composers created for each poem from the depths of their souls the one appropriate melody, inspired through and through and from beginning to end. How many operatic arias Handel transplanted into his oratorios! With what unconcern did Gluck use his half forgotten fashionable Italian operas for his later 'strictly dramatic' tragedies! Bach did such things less often, but the fact remains he *did* do them. Without injury to their ideals they were, indeed, all practical musicians who did not willingly allow one of their happiest inspirations to be lost." [1] It would be difficult to find a more reasonable statement about a question which has often bothered Bach enthusiasts. No doubt Hanslick bore it in mind when he made those borrowings from his own earlier writings to which I have already referred.

The tenor of Hanslick's criticism of Handel's music has been indicated in the short passage quoted from his remarks on "Alexander's Feast" and "Israel in Egypt" (see p. 45). A performance of the "Water Music" and "Fireworks Music" calls forth similar reflections on the obsolete nature of much of the music of that age. He remarks that the conductor, on

[1] *Fünf Jahre Musik*, p. 200.

the occasion of the performance of which he writes, wisely selected the most effective numbers (Overture, Adagio, Bourée, Andante, Menuet, Allegro) from the original twenty short movements of the "Water Music." He cannot help thinking on listening to these pieces how greatly the art of instrumental music has advanced since Handel's day. "The genius of Handel, the master of oratorio," he says, "is not to be found in his instrumental compositions. They betray all the crudity and ponderousness of an art just beginning to develop, without reaching the powerful originality of the works of Bach in this *genre*. We can much more easily delight in Handel's clavier suites than in this 'Celebrated Water Music,' the greater half of which is far from enjoyable. One sees its age in the whole work but not the genius of one of the greatest of his age. . . ." [1] Hanslick finds the "Fireworks Music" on the whole more interesting and a later notice of the G minor concerto (No. 10 of the twelve Concerti Grossi) runs: "In so far as Handel's instrumental works can be taken to represent the master of incomparably greater choral compositions, the G minor concerto is real and complete Handel. Without the depth and richness of combination of similar suites of Bach, the work yet possesses attractive and substantial ideas in an effective setting. . . . The first movement is a very serious Largo of beautiful breadth and

[1] *Aus dem Concertsaal*, p. 384.

fullness. It leads to a four-part fugal Allegro whose theme, rising chromatically and then spaced at wonderful intervals, in itself enhances the originality and difficulty of the composition. The third movement (the only one which leaves the tonic) is a Chaconne in E flat major with a continuous droning bass ('musette'), an exceedingly effective popular piece of graceful old-French character. According to Burney, this movement was always particularly in favour both with the composer and the public and was often inserted by Handel between the two parts of his oratorios. The short Allegro in three-eight time which follows it suited the Vienna public, contrary to expectation, even better, and had to be repeated. It appeals more through fine effects in the performance than through its actual content. . . ." [1]

[1] *Aus dem Concertsaal*, p. 421. The Burney reference is to his *Account of the Musical Performances ... in Commemoration of Handel* of which a German translation had been published in 1785.

CHAPTER VI

OF MOZART

"FOR my heart it begins with Mozart." I do not think it is overstressing this statement of Hanslick's if we allow ourselves to be guided by it to a special consideration of his views on Mozart's music. It will be remembered that the first opera Hanslick heard as a child was "The Magic Flute," and although his recollection of "Der Freischütz," which he first heard about the same time, was evidently more vivid, there can be no doubt that the early introduction to Mozart led to a discriminating enthusiasm for his works which is no less genuine because it happens to reflect the contemporary view on certain aspects of Mozart's operatic writing.

In the first volume of *Die Moderne Oper* there is an essay on the operas of Mozart. It is too long to translate in its entirety here, but as that part of it which deals with "Don Giovanni" gives a good idea of the kind of Mozartian Hanslick was, I think it worth a place at this point.

"The brilliant rainbow of Mozart's operas no longer shines complete on any single stage. Of the seven masterpieces which alone are meant when Mozart's operas are spoken of—*Idomeneo, Entführung, Figaro, Don Giovanni, Cosi fan tutte, The Magic Flute, Titus,*

—the first and the last are as good as forgotten. The *Entführung* and *Cosi fan tutte* appear every now and again, even if at long intervals, and with unequal and, particularly in the case of *Cosi fan tutte*, somewhat diminished effect. But the other three, *The Marriage of Figaro*, *Don Giovanni* and the *Magic Flute*, represent to-day the mainstay of every German opera house and adorn the best foreign stages. The admiration of the connoisseur and the delight of the public are merged into one and the effect of these works, even in weaker performances, is great, sure and inevitable. I will guard against being too discursive about three such wonderful works which the reader carries in head and heart from childhood's days. Only one confession I must make, and that is that *Don Giovanni* has retained completely for me its original power. Even now it fills me with new wonder and joy at each performance. Those who live for many years in almost uninterrupted association with music, experience a fading, complete or partial, of many of their earlier ideals; most often and most quickly in opera, that most transitory because most composite and least independent of all great music forms. With some of Mozart's operas, neither reverence for his name nor delight in the beauty of particular passages can deceive me into thinking that the whole work still lives with unimpaired strength; I cannot resist altogether the feeling of time's influence. Those who have experienced with me, in their impressionable youth, the enthusiasm for Beethoven and Weber, Schubert and Schumann, will understand that most readily. It was a happy and just enthusiasm which, however, easily led to coolness and injustice towards Mozart. In later years that is usually made good; one learns to thank Mozart anew and apologizes to him for foolish youthful judgments. Yet the rapid course of musical development and the general change of taste is not entirely without influence. The effectiveness of Mozart's music to-day varies in degree considerably. Graceful, noble, charming its effect will always be, but only at its highest points can it carry us away and thrill us to the marrow like a new revelation. Such a point is reached in *Don Giovanni*. No other opera, not even *Fidelio*, creates the same undiminished impression on me as this incredible union of the greatest musical beauty and dramatic originality. I have heard this work innumerable times, but when, after the stirring chorus of the first finale, the F major Andante begins hesitatingly in softly tapping triple measure, I must confess I am enchanted. This expression of lovely tenderness has never been surpassed. And when in the last scene the guest of stone enters Don Juan's room, his mighty call gives me a shudder as if I were hearing it for the first time, and I am conscious anew that no one but Mozart has given expression to the superhuman with such staggering power.

"I will not dwell here on the numerous new translations, stage suggestions etc. which already constitute a small library. Many of them might with advantage be put into practice, but Mozart's *Don Giovanni*, when all is said and done, still has its wonderful effect without any of these improvements. Only two important points I should like to touch on, two traditions of stage practice which custom has justified and for which I would put in a word even against Mozart himself. I refer to the closing section of the first finale and the almost universally omitted original finale of the second act. The second finale was heard once in Vienna in a simple concert performance. Known to very few of the audience from the score its existence had remained a secret to many. In Mozart's original score, after Don Giovanni's descent to hell with which the opera closes in our performances, Donna Anna appears on the scene with Ottavio, Elvira, Zerlina, and Masetto looking for Don Giovanni, whose dreadful end is related to them by Leporello. Whereupon Donna Anna and Ottavio announce in a delicate duet their forthcoming marriage and join with the others in the edifying moral

> "Luck in vice like smoke blows past
> A speedy life brings death as fast"

Mozart himself cut the greater part of this finale for the Vienna performance, a cut which even Otto

Jahn regards as 'really an improvement.' We will not be more Mozartian than Mozart or Jahn and readily dispense with this second finale which, after the most magnificent scene in the opera, sounds very conventional and weakens both musically and dramatically the impression of what precedes it. In Berlin, when Jenny Lind sang as guest, this finale, which had up to then been suppressed, was completely restored. It was soon necessary, however, to return to the former custom because the public, according to Gumprecht, acting on a natural feeling, left the house after Don Giovanni's descent and so, on its own authority, made the opera end at the point demanded by æsthetic necessity. In Prague I myself witnessed years ago the same experiment carried out by the Conservatoire and experienced, in complete agreement with the audience, the cooling effect of this original ending.

"There is yet another part of *Don Giovanni* which is everywhere performed in a manner contradictory to Mozart's original score and which Alfred von Wolzogen, likewise in vain, insists on attempting to have produced literally. It is the finale of the first act which, in the original, is written for soloists only, without choir. After Zerlina has been rescued and Elvira, Anna and Ottavio have unmasked, the whole chorus (according to Mozart) should leave the stage. If, in accordance with the desires of Wolzogen and

Jahn, the original were restored and the chorus done away with, then one of the most powerful effects of the end of this act would be sacrificed. Apart from the greater dramatic probability, that the people would not leave the hall at the most exciting moment, but would rather back up Zerlina and Masetto against Don Giovanni, the power of the raging chorus 'Trema, trema, scelerato!' is musically irreplaceable and, for those who have once experienced it, not to be sacrificed. It is a remarkable thing that in the staging of these two finales the general instinct for the effective and the appropriate has come up against the indisputable letter of the original, and everywhere, without any specific agreement, as if compelled by a natural law, has been upheld. On the smallest stages and on the largest, in the whole of Germany, France, Italy, in London and St. Petersburg, *Don Giovanni* is performed with the chorus in the first finale and without the sextet in the second finale. What has been maintained for half a century with such unanimity throughout the world, has surely a proper basis in feeling. And now it even has a historical justification the ignoring of which seems almost as inadmissable as a deliberate alteration of Mozart's score."

The long article on Mozart's "Don Giovanni," written on the occasion of the "Jubilee" of the opera, was reprinted in *Musikalisches und Litterarisches*, and contains amongst other things an account of the scene in the second act between Leporello and Zerlina which has almost always been omitted and which Dr. Alfred Einstein seems to have proved to be spurious.[1] Hanslick's account of it concludes thus: "And now Zerlina comes back and brings with her Donna Elvira. Both are astonished to find the criminal has escaped and suppose he has been set free by his master. Zerlina goes off again to acquaint Ottavio with this incident; Elvira remains behind alone and sings at this point her wonderful aria (composed for the Vienna performance), 'Mi tradì quell'alma ingrata,' which, as is well known, is now transferred to the first act. Leporello's aria after the sextet, his duet with Zerlina and the all too farcical chair scene were suppressed in Vienna soon after the first performances. We can hardly complain; these scenes retard considerably the already somewhat slowly moving action of the second act, and are musically of little value.

"Of greater importance is the dispute about another generally omitted number, the second half of the last finale." Here follows a literal transcription of the passage beginning, "In Mozart's original score, after Don Giovanni's descent to hell," etc., from the earlier article. One or two small alterations are made in the manner to which I have already referred. But in this case, small as they are, they seem to have more

[1] See *Music and Letters*, October, 1938.

significance than usual, and I will take the opportunity of giving them in some detail. The passage in
the original article from "Mozart himself cut the
greater part," etc., to "than Mozart or Jahn" is altered
in the later version to the more accurate statement,
"This closing scene was, it is true, included in the
first Vienna performances, but very soon left out
altogether, without doubt in Mozart's lifetime and
with his foreknowledge. It immediately became the
general practice to close the opera with the descent of
Don Giovanni." Thereafter for *gern*, which I have
translated "readily," Hanslick now substitutes the
slightly stronger *willig*, "willingly." Instead of
abschwägt (weakens) he writes *verflacht* (flattens) and
puts in "deep" in front of "impression." The sentence
about Jenny Lind now reads "tried to restore."
Bald (soon) is replaced by *alsbald* (at once); "according to Gumprecht" is omitted. The sentence about
Prague is shortened to "In a festival performance at
Prague many years ago I made the same observation."
The succeeding passage about the use of chorus is
verbally somewhat transposed and extended. To
"the desires of Wolzogen and Jahn" is added "and
others" and "the full throated jubilation of 'Viva la
libertà' " is instanced in addition to "Trema, trema,
scelerata" as a chorus not to be dispensed with. The
next two sentences contain only minor verbal alterations, apparently quite insignificant, but after "with

the chorus in the first finale and without the sextet
in the second finale" Hanslick has added the emphatic,
"Und dabei mag es auch bleiben" (And so may it
continue), which seems to gain added point as the
tailpiece to the repetition, with added emphasis, of
an opinion expressed thirteen years before.

After this lengthy quotation it is not difficult to
foresee that some will consider I have all but given
away my case for Hanslick as a Mozartian by revealing
his attitude to the final ensemble of "Don Giovanni."
To those I would point out, first, that it is surely
unreasonable to expect Hanslick, living in the midst
of strong romantic influence, to make a plea for the
restoration of a seemingly purely formal finale which,
by common consent, was omitted everywhere. And,
in the second place, this emphatic agreement with the
practice of omitting the finale proves that Hanslick
was far from attaching no importance to considerations other than purely musical, when such considerations were appropriate. If he had had no use for
anything but "the idea of form moving in sound" [1]
it would have been a matter of complete indifference
to him whether the finale was dramatically right or
not so long as it was performed according to the
written instructions of the composer. And if he had
then still disliked it, it would have been for purely
musical and not dramatic reasons.

[1] Alfred Einstein, *A Short History of Music*, p. 201.

The following article on one of Mozart's Divertimenti, written for the *Neue Freie Presse* in 1866,[1] will serve to supplement the impression given by the "Don Giovanni" criticism: "Hellmesberger's second quartet evening began with Schubert's G major quartet, a work which, revealing in some places all Schubert's richness, makes up for direct imitation of Beethovenish idiosyncrasies at others by its own strength and freshness. A Divertimento of Mozart's for string quartet and two horns in B flat was, strangely enough, labelled 'new,' and had in fact not been heard in Vienna before. Of the large number of Mozart's Divertimenti, Serenades, Cassations and suchlike, which were mostly composed hastily to order and clearly show their origin as Society Music (Gesellschaftsmusik), two works stand out as masterpieces, the Divertimento just mentioned (K. No. 287) and another in D major (K. No. 334) already played by Hellmesberger. The 'Andante with Variations' from the latter was also performed at the last Philharmonic Concert. The new Divertimento gave us the greatest pleasure from beginning to end. It goes without saying that the cardinal virtues of Mozart— clearness, euphony, and beauty of form—were not lacking. But there are amongst Mozart's youthful and occasional compositions many which, in spite of these never failing merits, reveal too little inspiration

[1] Reprinted in *Aus dem Concertsaal*, p. 389.

and idea-content still to charm us nowadays,—just as many of Haydn's works which should be called insignificant, boring and antiquated are described in such conventional phrases as 'perpetually youthful.' Unfortunately such indiscriminate praise only damages those works of the master which stand out fresh and charming in a bed of smaller or half-withered flowers. The sextet in B flat is one of the outstanding works. One can hear that it was written with keenness and joy and the same keenness and joy overflow into the heart of the untroubled listener. No one expects great pathos, passion or dramatic flashes; the Divertimento never belies its character of Society Music, of musical 'entertainment.' The 'concertante' nature of the first violin part, which leads the most piquant conversation not without coquetry, the close sequence of the six movements and finally the decking out of the quartet-like piece with two low horns all stamp it with that unmistakable physiognomy. The two low B flat horns, confined to natural tones, do not actually enter into the structure of the musical thought, but they lend to the whole a charming colour and fullness of tone. This fresh and acceptable sound of the horns, peacefully moving at the simplest intervals, gives the picture a somewhat idyllic, serenade-like character. We think involuntarily of garden-music and ornamental rococo pavilions with lighted windows; below in the park, ladies in rustling silk and powdered hair, and gentlemen with fine features and gay-coloured costumes. All this in the idealizing charm of a strange and yet near past, without any touch of the ridiculous which those manners and times so easily assume for us. On those painted fans and lace cuffs tears of joy and sorrow fell then as now, and under the high gold-embroidered lace bodices of the last century hearts beat in hate and in love as they do to-day. Mozart's 'Divertimento' works like a spell restoring a piece of life that is past."

There is one other passage amongst Hanslick's concert notices which seems specially worthy of inclusion at this point. It is in rather a different category from the previous quotations, being almost in the nature of an "interview." On the occasion of the Mozart birth centenary in 1856 Mozart's son Karl, by then a man of seventy-two, was present and spoke a few words to Hanslick. It is not easy to think of this old man as the son of one of the world's greatest composers who died quite young. As no person or thing connected with Mozart can be quite lacking in interest and as I have not seen, in the Mozart literature generally available, any account of this meeting of Karl Mozart and Hanslick, I will give it here in full as related by Hanslick.[1]

"Among the guests the chief object of general

[1] *Aus dem Concertsaal*, p. 112. The passage is used again practically verbatim in *Aus meinem Leben*, p. 293. Karl Mozart died in 1858.

curiosity and interest was Karl Mozart, son of the great composer. Of Mozart's two sons Karl is the elder; the younger one, who bore his father's baptismal name and had likewise devoted himself to music, died, as is well known, some years ago in Karlsbad. Karl Mozart, a slender little man with dark eyes and slightly white hair, simple and extremely modest in manner, was only seven years old when he lost his father. Nevertheless he assured me, when I questioned him, that he had a very lively recollection of his father and remembered two things in particular. First that Mozart had to look after him a great deal and take him regularly for walks as mother Constanze at that time had long been ailing and kept indoors. And second, that he was often taken by his father to the theatre, a pleasure which, strangely enough, he never sought later. When fifteen years old he went to a firm of merchants in Italy and later entered a government department. He was a clerk in the Department of Finance and now lives on a pension. As he spent nearly all his life in Italy he considers himself almost an Italian, and even speaks somewhat broken German with an Italian accent. Karl Mozart never married, and as his brother also left no children the name of the great master dies with him. 'That would only be a pity,' said the modest man, 'if the sons had inherited their father's talent. As it is, it matters little.' He did not or would not consider how we cherish with

F 2

double tenderness the heirs of a great man who, during his lifetime, did not find a due measure of love and recognition. Karl Mozart listened to the music calmly; no longer accustomed to concerts, he found, as is easily understood, the amount of music offered on Sunday too great. When I heard that Mozart's son wished to be present in person at the Salzburg Festival I was somewhat alarmed as I thought how formidable and dangerous the effect of such a festival must be on the mind of a seventy-year-old man. It has always for me been one of the most touching experiences when thousands unite jubilantly in the praise of one man. Each feels proud when he belongs to the nation of the immortal one; prouder still the lucky citizen who even began his life in the same town. What a colossal flood of feelings, then, will break over that man whose spirit must bear all the jubilation with the thought, 'He was my father!' "[1]

[1] Since the first edition of this book the above passage (up to "he never sought later") has been given in almost identical translation in O. E. Deutsch's *Mozart —A Documentary Biography* (London 1965). But, curiously, it is quoted as an anonymous extract from *Blätter fur Musik, Theater und Kunst* (Vienna 1856), and even then, "second-hand," as it were, from Rudolf von Lewicki's *Mozarteums-Mitteilungen* Vol. II (Salzburg 1919). There is, however, no doubt that Hanslick must be credited with the original.

CHAPTER VII

OF BEETHOVEN

AMONGST many notices by Hanslick of performances of the music of Beethoven there are three which I think stand out as specially interesting. The first deals with the Eighth Symphony and is dated 1864. It is of particular interest because of its bearing on Hanslick's attitude to so-called "interpretation" of Beethoven's music. The second is an account of a performance of the "Eroica" under Wagner in 1872 and the third mentions an interesting detail in Brahms's presentation of the Missa Solemnis in 1873.

"It is very gratifying that the eighth symphony, which has for long been persistently neglected, is at last appearing more frequently on concert programmes. Oulibicheff was certainly completely justified when he called the eighth symphony 'la moins goûtée' of the nine sisters. It has been ignored to such an extent that in the Vienna programmes of the thirties and even the forties we find the Pastoral Symphony described simply as 'Symphony in F major by Beethoven' just as if Beethoven had written no other symphony in F major. The eighth symphony seemed by its peculiar position to confuse the public and the critics. It inclined to the first two symphonies by its modest proportions and at the same time numerous characteristics (notably in the last movement) indicated the style of the third period. The proximity on the one hand of the seventh symphony with its overflowing vigour and on the other of the gigantic ninth, had an adverse effect on it. Moreover, in its pure musical objectivity (a characteristic shared with the fourth symphony) it offered little opportunity for poetic interpretation to commentators already spoilt by the habit of picture seeking. What heterogeneous interpretations has this stubborn eighth had to put up with! Lenz sees in it 'military' ideas; the finale is for him 'a tattoo created with the greatest poesy.' His countryman Oulibicheff offers an incredible explanation of the charming Allegretto by taking it in all seriousness as an intentional satire on Rossini's music of which he supposes Beethoven wished to make fun. Less daring interpreters have searched spasmodically in Beethoven's utterances and in the incidents of his life for a poetic key to the locked-up meaning of the eighth symphony, and renewed their lamentations that Beethoven did not carry out his project—alleged to have been communicated to Schindler—of indicating by titles and short suggestions the 'poetic idea' of his compositions. We took the liberty once of regarding it as a real piece of good fortune that this plan was never carried out,[1] a heresy

[1] Those who would like to know the depths of pseudo-scholarship which can be reached by one evidently intent on

for which we had to suffer at that time. We were filled with great joy to find in a critique of Otto Jahn's on the new edition of Beethoven, the same conviction fully set forth. Jahn illustrates the uncertainty of that intention, no doubt only fleetingly considered by Beethoven, and reminds us of several examples. For instance, asked once by Schindler about the meaning of the Sonatas in D minor and F minor, Beethoven said, 'Just read Shakespeare's "Tempest".' Jahn remarks on this, 'It is certainly not without interest that this particular drama could inspire Beethoven to such creations, but to look for the explanation of these works in Shakespeare would only attest to the impotence of the musical conception.' Even when Beethoven gives a more exact reference the understanding of the music will not be increased. His trusted friend Amenda relates that Beethoven said to him that in the Adagio of the F major Quartet (Op. 18 No. 1) the churchyard scene in 'Romeo and Juliet' floated before his eyes. Will the man who reads carefully his Shakespeare and tries to visualize it at a performance of the Adagio, will he, I ask, have his enjoyment of the piece heightened or disturbed? It is asserted that Beethoven in the last movement of the D minor Sonata had in mind a

making good Beethoven's omission should read *Beethoven und die Dichtung* by Arnold Schering; or Dr. Einstein's review of the book in *Music and Letters*, April, 1937, will do.

rider at the gallop, and in the first movement of the violin concerto the impatient knocking of one vainly seeking entrance late at night. It is possible that a pregnant and suggestive impression at the right moment called forth a characteristic motive. But the outer stimulus has nothing to do with the artistic development of this germ, with the creative organization of the work of art. The activity of the artist belongs to quite another realm and whoever believes that a work of art is put together out of accidental outer causes, has no idea of artistic creation. Should anyone, for example, hit on the idea of deriving the first movement of the violin concerto in its psychological development and external composition from that given situation of knocking by night, then for heaven's sake let him go on knocking; the door of understanding will not be opened to him. 'Titles and notes, even if authentic and originating from Beethoven himself, would not appreciably advance our knowledge of the sense and meaning of the work of art. It is much more to be feared that they would give rise to misunderstandings and falsities in the same way as those Beethoven made public have already done. We can therefore be content that Beethoven did not always give verbal explanations which might have led too many people into the mistake of thinking that because they understood the title they could also understand the work. His music says all he wished to say, it is and remains the open spring from which each one who is receptive can create.' Such words cannot be too often repeated or too widely spread." [1]

The notice of Wagner's conducting of the "Eroica" begins with some remarks about Wagner's statements in *Uber das Dirigiren* about this symphony. Hanslick points out that it is unreasonable to regard as unsound all performances of the "Eroica" *not* conducted by Wagner. He regards Wagner's performance as mainly intended to be a demonstration of the one true way of conducting the work—seeing that it is one of the works most often performed in Vienna, and that Wagner has published such individual views about it. He sees no reason, however, why Wagner's performance should be considered any more authoritative than those of Herbeck and Dessoff. "The novelty in Wagner's interpretation of the Eroica," he continues, "consists, in short, in frequent 'modification of the tempo' of each movement. With that favourite expression and this second one, 'proper conception of the Melos,' which is to be the actual key to the right tempo, Wagner indicates the reforms he requires of others and practises himself in the performance of the symphonies of Beethoven. There are movements where in fact the 'dynamic monotony' that is so hated by Wagner can be enlivened and inter-

[1] *Aus dem Concertsaal*, pp. 318-320.

rupted without any disadvantage. Such a movement is the finale of the Eroica where the construction is that of extended variation form which undoubtedly admits of a characteristic tempo modification in each variation of the theme. A set of variations played through at the same tempo easily stiffens into uninspired formalism. And in this very movement Wagner's changing speeds have a delightful effect. At other places Wagner seems to us to go too far with his modifications. For example, after beginning the first movement at a very quick tempo, he takes the second motive (*dolce*, bar 45) noticeably slower, whereby the listener not yet quite introduced to the basic nature of the movement is confused and the 'heroic' character of the symphony is diverted into sentimentality. Wagner takes the Scherzo very fast, all too *presto*, a piece of daring which can be dangerous even for a virtuoso orchestra. The Funeral March sounded wonderfully beautiful especially in the gradual dying away of the main theme. The whole performance was, as I have said, of the greatest interest, full of fine features and effects. For all that, hardly anyone doubted that these 'modifications' were more Wagner's than Beethoven's.

"Some bold deviations from the general rule will succeed so well with an original and gifted personality that only pedantic narrow-mindedness would take offence at them. But there is nothing more dangerous than to generalize from an exceptionally gifted case and to propound as an unconditional rule a purely individual conception. If Wagner's principles of conducting were generally adopted the door would be opened to an unbearable arbitrariness in the changing of tempo; we would soon have no longer symphonies by Beethoven but symphonies 'freely adapted from Beethoven,' which would present a different appearance in every town and under every conductor. The wretched 'tempo rubato,' that musical sea-sickness which spoils the performances of so many singers and virtuosi and against which only our orchestral performances offer an adequate antidote and tonic, would also immediately take possession of them. And thus the last stronghold of our public musical life would be destroyed. Wagner acts as a conductor in the same way as he acts as composer. What his individual originality dictates and his quite exceptional talent brings off, is to be the general principle of art, the one true and authorized method. Out of his extremely personal poetic-painting-musical gift he abstracts for himself a new theory of opera which leads him to original and brilliant accomplishments, to compositions which find their justification in their inspired subjectivity, and are effective because they are Wagnerian. Wagner, however, does not content himself with that, but condemns every other operatic style as a 'colossal mistake,' not seeing that his own opera style in the hands of any other becomes caricature. As soon as all opera composers write in the style of 'Tristan and Isolde' we listeners will all wander into the lunatic asylum, and if Wagner's 'tempo modifications' gain complete possession of our orchestras then conductors, violinists and wind-instrumentalists will soon follow us there." [1]

The passage about Brahms's conducting of the Missa Solemnis is comparatively short, and deals only with one detail of the performance, but it is a detail which shows the difference between the desire for pedantic accuracy and the insistence of Brahms's creative mind on the observation and emphasis of an essential point in the score. Here is Hanslick's account of the performance: [2]

"Enough has already been written about Beethoven's Mass in D, that gigantic creation with its sublime beauty, profound intention and characteristic Beethovenish violence. One single detail of importance must on this occasion be mentioned. The last movement (Dona nobis pacem), surely the most inspired of all, was performed quite correctly for the first time by Brahms. In the twenty-ninth bar from the end (page 296 of the Schott score) and

---

[1] *Concerte, Componisten und Virtuosen der letzten fünfzehn Jahre*, pp. 49–50.
[2] *Ibid.*, pp. 81–82.

onwards from there the drum is accustomed to strike A, evidently under the misconception that the tuning indicated at the beginning of the movement B-flat-F should, in the D major section, be changed to D-A, and that the B flat in the last twenty-nine bars of the Mass is a misprint for A. But at the beginning of the Agnus Dei the instruction is 'Tympani in B flat and F' and nowhere throughout the whole section is this contradicted. The B flat on page 296 seq. is therefore no misprint. Is it not remarkable that so considerable an error should have persisted through decades and should even have been adopted by musicians like Nottebohm and Julius Stern[1] in whose pianoforte arrangements of the Mass the wrong note A is to be found? Brahms has now restored the original text, if one can put it thus, when all that is required is that what is written in the score should be properly read and played. The boldness with which the B flat of the drum enters and forms the foundation of the following chords is magnificent in its effect. Brahms made it greater still by reinforcing the B flat of the drum with the double basses *pizzicato*. It is to be hoped that his procedure will remain as an example from now on."

[1] This has been corrected in the modern Peters edition of Stern's piano arrangement of Beethoven's *Missa Solemnis*.

CHAPTER VIII

GESCHICHTE DES CONCERTWESENS

TWO short extracts may now be given from one of
Hanslick's books which is in rather a different
category from the bulk of his work. The *Geschichte
des Concertwesens in Wien* is the title often given to
two volumes of which only the first really bears it.
It is true that in the volume entitled *Aus dem Concertsaal*, from which I have already quoted, Hanslick
indicates in a preface that it may be regarded as a
continuation of the *Geschichte* as it is indeed a record
of concert-giving in Vienna brought up to date. But
Aus dem Concertsaal is more than that, and is chiefly
interesting not so much as a record but as a series of
brilliant criticisms. The first volume makes, by
comparison, rather heavy reading and is better
regarded as a valuable reference book. It is indeed a
record of concerts given in Vienna and of the music
performed at them from about 1750 to 1869, the year
of publication. Apart from *Vom Musikalisch-Schönen*
it is in fact Hanslick's only planned book. By its very
nature it required a great deal of laborious research,
and the documentation is carefully provided in
detailed footnotes. The history of the various concert-
giving bodies in Vienna is given with the names of
all distinguished performers, the dates of their con-

certs, and some extracts from contemporary criticism. The two passages which I propose to give here will serve the double purpose of giving some idea of the nature of the book and of indicating Hanslick's attitude to the music of Schumann. After some account of the "interest and attention" aroused by the novelty of David's and Berlioz's music, Hanslick goes on to say: "Robert Schumann, in whom there was more genius and artistry than in ten Berlioz's and Davids put together, experienced soon after this an undeniable fiasco with two of his most beautiful compositions, the B flat Symphony and the Pianoforte Concerto in A minor. Both were received in the hall of the Musikverein on January 1st 1847 with respectful silence. Schumann himself conducted but the respect was for his wife. He himself was almost as unknown as Berlioz who, up to the time of his first concert, had been constantly confused with the violinist Bériot. Although Schumann could boast of almost ten years of distinction as composer and writer, although he had formerly actually lived in Vienna for a time and published several pieces there, he was still unknown to the Viennese. No one took any notice of him, no one put a song, a pianoforte piece or a symphony of his on any programme. When Schumann visited Vienna with his wife in 1846, he was only spoken of as 'the husband of Clara Wieck' and his few adherents trembled lest there should be a repetition of the incident which took place at a foreign Court-concert where his Highness after many courtesies to Clara Schumann asked our master most graciously, 'Are you also musical?' "

At this point Hanslick has the following footnote: "The Viennese journalists seem also to have had no idea at that time of Schumann's importance. The press either took no notice of him or else was mildly derogatory. The *Wiener Musikzeitung* had a few encouraging but inadequate lines about Robert Schumann after Clara's third concert. The essay 'Robert Schumann' in Frankl's *Sontagsblättern* (No. 49 of the year 1846) by the author of this book was the first to draw the attention of the Viennese public to Schumann's high standing and to his most significant works. Still earlier in an article ' *Robert Schumann and his cantata "Paradies und Peri"* ' (in No. 59 of the Prague newspaper *Ost und West* of 1846) the author had attempted to spread the knowledge and appreciation of Schumann's compositions." [1]

In a later passage [2] Hanslick says: "The reception and appreciation of Mendelssohn in Vienna had not been very rapid. Schumann's adoption was still slower. Not only were no traces left behind of his appearance as a young composer in 1844 but in the winter of 1846–47 he was in Vienna in vain with his admirable

[1] *Geschichte des Concertwesens in Wien*, p. 371.
[2] *Ibid.*, p. 428.

wife. We have seen how timidly the *Gesellschaft der Musikfreunde* introduced the first work of Schumann (the C major Symphony) in December 1854, how slowly they proceeded to the B flat and D minor Symphonies (1856 and 1857) and finally in 1858 ventured 'Paradise and the Peri' which was already a favourite work throughout Germany and had even been performed in American towns. The following year Herbeck (considerably ˉassisted by the Singverein) introduced 'Vom Pagen und der Königstöchter' (1850); in 1859 for the first time with tremendous effect 'Manfred' (Lewinsky recited the verses particularly well) and finally the music to Goethe's 'Faust,' first the third part in 1860 and then in 1863, with Stockhausen's incomparable assistance, all three parts. In the year 1862 'Peri' was repeated and in 1863 'Manfred.' These works have now become necessities of our musical life. The public has overcome, through closer acquaintance, the strangeness and illusive nature of Schumann's music and, at the same time, corrected that misconception whereby for a long time Schumann was numbered with Liszt and Wagner among the purveyors of 'The Music of the Future.' There can be no doubt that that view considerably impeded the progress of Schumann's music with the 'classical' majority of our public."

These extracts will serve to illustrate the nature of this painstaking book of Hanslick's which, in the earlier editions of *Grove's Dictionary*, was specially noted as being indispensible to students of the history of music. The volume is indeed packed with interesting details regarding the first performances of works now in the established repertoire of symphony and chamber concerts, particular attention being given to Beethoven and Schubert. It is, however, less a book to read than to refer to and I am inclined to suspect that the number of times it is consulted and drawn upon is greater than the number of acknowledgments to it seen in print.

CHAPTER IX

HANSLICK IN ENGLAND

IT seems strange that although the fact that Hanslick acted as juror for the musical department of the Exhibitions of Paris (1867 and 1868) and of Vienna (1873 and 1892) is mentioned in the *Musical Times* obituary and in Grove, no mention is made of Hanslick's first visit to London in the same capacity in 1862 nor of his subsequent visit in 1886. His duties were to adjudicate along with others on the merits of the various instruments exhibited. It is interesting to note, by the way, that these included horns made of aluminium which Hanslick commended on account of the possibility of effecting a reduction of weight to be carried by military bandsmen! The metal was too expensive at that time to be used generally but, by the time he is writing *Aus meinem Leben*, aluminium has become so much cheaper that Hanslick thinks Besson's invention might be used profitably.

There are many entertaining details of these visits to England, which included an excursion to Oxford and a day at Epsom for "The Derby"! These took place during the first visit of eight weeks in May and June, 1862. It was then also that Hanslick met Dickens, an occasion more memorable for him than any of his meetings with London musicians. He had been a keen reader of Dickens's works and looked forward to the prospect of one of his famous readings. Joachim introduced him to the painter Lehmann, at whose house a small party was given, the "six or eight guests" including Hanslick, Wilkie Collins, Dickens and his daughter.

"Dickens, then fifty, was jovial and unceremonious in his behaviour; there was in his irregular mobile face something of the genial comedian. It could have been no news for him to hear of the enormous popularity of his works in Germany, yet he was glad to hear of it from me. He sent me a few days later a ticket for one of his readings in the St. James Hall with a charming letter which occupies a place of honour in my little collection of autographs. This collection consists only of letters addressed to me. I never was a collector of autographs although of all collecting passions that is the one for which I have by far the most sympathy. The only one I cannot understand is postage-stamp collecting.[1]

"Dickens's reading made on me a quite original and pleasantly homely impression. It took place at eight o'clock in the evening, nevertheless without the compulsion of the otherwise inevitable evening dress.

[1] There is an amusing parallel to this in Tovey's essay on Gluck in the *Heritage of Music:* "I have often envied the connoisseurship of a philatelist, but nobody wants to know what it feels like to have a mind that has never contemplated a larger field than that of a postage-stamp."

Dickens, with a black tie, a carnation in his comfortable morning-coat, stood at a little table with green draperies and read some selected chapters from his 'Copperfield.' They were all favourite figures and scenes to a public which knew the context exactly. Dickens spoke in an effortless, mostly humorous tone, simply yet virtuosically. His living, dramatic delivery moved the audience alternately to sadness and laughter. His listeners, almost exclusively of homely middle-class people full of devotion, hung on his words and applauded warm-heartedly. A salutary spectacle of national respect and love! Such a thing would be unthinkable in Germany. Where should we find a novelist so popular that he could attract a big public each winter by reading some well-known chapters from his works, and, like Dickens, in spite of the low prices of admission, make a considerable profit? Dickens told me that he had been offered for six readings in Australia, the enormous sum of ten thousand pounds, but he could not make up his mind to the journey."

Of Hanslick's second visit to London there is a more detailed account from a musical point of view in his book *Musikalisches Skizzenbuch*. Richter's and Sullivan's Symphony concerts are contrasted, to the detriment, of course, of Sullivan, but the latter's "Mikado" is greatly appreciated. The Italian Opera at Covent Garden is reviewed in detail, but by no means enthusiastically. Indeed the position of opera in London leads Hanslick to a consideration of English opera generally, and it is here that we find a passage which might well have been written by Sir Thomas Beecham in our own day. I feel it must be translated here.

"It must be said that England cannot reach the same level as other musical nations so long as London has no permanent opera playing throughout the year. I mean, of course, not a theatre only for original operas by English composers but one in which, in addition to these, the best from the classical and modern repertoire of German, French and Italian operas will be performed. Such an established opera house should not be exclusively for the aristocracy but must aim rather at finished ensemble than at providing expensive 'stars.' It would have a most salutary effect on the musical education of the English public which either does not know the best foreign operas at all or else only hears occasional performances of a haphazard nature. It would also be the best if not the only encouragement for English composers who at present do not lightly undertake the composition of an opera which at best can have only five or six performances. And finally, it would constitute the most urgent complement to the frightfully increasing number of Conservatoires and Musical Schools in London; it would be the longed-for haven for innumerable trained singers and instrumentalists who, year after year, pour forth from these institutions to find no employment. A permanent opera house in London deserves the most liberal support of society and of the government, deserves it far more than the 'Royal College' and the 'Royal Academy' and whatever all the other training centres are called, which produce an enormous artist-proletariat who as fledglings can find no food. I repeat, the establishment of a permanent opera in London is the first, the most important thing which England must do for its musical reputation, its musical dignity."[1]

[1] Opera was finally established in England, one hopes, by the formation of the Covent Garden Opera Co. in 1945, later to become The Royal Opera. The Sadler's Wells Opera Co. which had done so much since 1931 for opera in English, took up its home at The London Coliseum in 1968.

CHAPTER X

BILLROTH AND BRAHMS

HANSLICK'S greatest friends were Billroth and Brahms. Brahms is more widely known than Billroth nowadays, and it is inevitable that Hanslick's friendly relations with him should be better known than his equally close, if not even closer friendship with Theodor Billroth, the distinguished surgeon and keen amateur musician. Most of Brahms's biographers have indicated the strong bond that existed between Billroth and Brahms and have referred to Billroth's share in providing opportunities for many of the first performances of Brahms's chamber music. Similarly there is plenty of evidence readily available of Hanslick's appreciation of Brahms and his works. But to get an idea of the very close friendship of Hanslick and Billroth we must go to Hanslick's autobiography and to the correspondence that passed between them, some of which forms an appendix to the second volume of the autobiography. There was evidently a rare sympathy between these two men which united them from the moment Billroth first visited Hanslick in Vienna in 1867 till the eminent surgeon's much lamented death in 1894. In the midst of an extremely busy life Billroth yet found time to write to Hanslick about the performances he heard and Hanslick tells us how often he played the new works of Brahms in duet form with Billroth. Billroth's home was the scene of many performances by Brahms with members of the Hellmesberger Quartet; Saint-Saens, Amalie Joachim and George Henschel also performed there.

There is no mistaking the warm tones of affection in which Hanslick speaks of Billroth. Their musical tastes were similar and Billroth was even more intolerant of Wagner's ideas than Hanslick himself. Many extracts in English from Billroth's collected letters are to be found in the various Brahms biographies, especially in that of Florence May. Hanslick's selection consists mainly of letters with some definite æsthetic or philosophic interest, and especially those which have a bearing on Billroth's one essay on music, "Who is Musical?" The essay remained unfinished, but it was left in Hanslick's keeping, and he wrote an introduction to it and had it published. Indeed it was largely owing to Hanslick that the existing part of it took shape at all, as Billroth required a good deal of persuasion to embark upon the task. It was not that the desire was lacking, but that he felt himself insufficiently equipped musically to undertake a thorough investigation of the problem of musicality. Also he was too much of a scientist to take for granted things which required proving or to allow himself to indulge in vague generalizations where positive research was called for. As he said himself, "In the writings of others I readily overlook inaccuracies if the personality of the writer attracts me; in my own writing I must carefully weigh every sentence." Every new aspect of his subject led him to seemingly endless study, and he despaired of ever being able to sift his reading and his experience sufficiently to make a readable treatise. Hanslick kept insisting that as surgeon and musician he was doubly equipped to investigate the nature of musical talent, and so at last Billroth handed over to Hanslick his musical-physiological study as far as it went. It cannot be said to answer definitely the question it poses. How could it? But in the examination of the question it ranges over a wide field which includes the more scientific aspects of the subject—acoustics and the nature of the human ear—and the more complicated æsthetic problems of music—its connection with the other arts and with nature.

Some idea of his deep regard for Hanslick may perhaps best be gathered from the last letter Billroth wrote to him. Billroth was already seriously ill; he died a month later.

". . . My poor worn out heart works with such difficulty to pass on the blood stream flowing to it that I feel its groaning. How long must I carry on this drudgery? My strength is at an end. Then comes the digitalis whip! This can't last much longer. On this New Year's Eve I dreamt once again that dream I've had so often, that I was dissecting my own body. No more of that! Away with such thoughts! Only to a true friend dare one betray such moments of weakness. I know that you too often have to suffer much, but you are much braver than I am and say nothing about it.

"A thousand thanks, dear friend, for sending me again a most interesting piece of your 'Life.' I devoured it greedily of course, I seem to be a cannibal. To write about Brahms is very difficult, especially for you with your predominating south-German feeling, in spite of your birthplace Prague. A friend must write about a living friend! Everything can't, won't and shouldn't be said. 'No man can see into another' used to be a favourite saying of Brahms's.

"I believe that people are often enough mistaken about me too. They take me for a person of an energetic disposition, always striving after new creative activity. It's quite the opposite. I am actually a Baltic herring, sentimental through and through; a Hamlet-nature, only by outward conditions and self-discipline achieving energetic action with a struggle. Only when things can't be reversed, ambition and vanity prevent me taking back my word and then, with the utmost inner goading, I am pushed gasping into action. Funny isn't it?

"Admittedly I was born in Pomerania, but all

my grandparents had Swedish blood and a dash of French came from my great-grandmother (Beaulieu). I'm an extraordinary mongrel, bred and brought up in the land of Ernst Moritz Arndt. This business of races and descent from them is a curious thing, almost as complicated as that about major and minor or common time and three-four time. What is one to do with these often not at all bad products, partly major and partly minor, or neither one nor the other, sometimes in common and sometimes in three-four time? I've given up trying to find even conventional laws about such things. . . ."

Specht gives first-hand recollections of the "Triumvirate," as he calls it—the term was also used by Hanslick himself. He was, as I have already indicated, sympathetic to neither Hanslick nor Billroth. Brahms and his music are his real subject, and he suggests that neither of these friends had an adequate appreciation of the composer. He speaks of Hanslick's "determinedly reverent attitude" to Brahms's works and says that his criticisms were "based on reason rather than on emotion." It is noticeable, however, that Specht seems only to quote Hanslick at his most luke-warm or unresponsive. He makes much, for instance, of Hanslick's initial lack of appreciation of the A major pianoforte quartet. This indeed seems a curious lapse on Hanslick's part. But one must remember that this work was being heard for the first time, and it would surely have been more curious, not to say suspicious, if Hanslick's criticisms had been consistently appreciative. Specht does not quote Hanslick's enthusiastic account of, for example, the D minor violin Sonata or the "Zigeunerlieder." He quotes an adverse remark which he says Hanslick made after hearing a first performance on two pianos of the Fourth Symphony, but he does not mention Hanslick's highly appreciative account of the work published in *Aus dem Tagebuche eines Musikers*. He shows that Hanslick was doubtful about certain aspects of the violin concerto, calls him "a veritable Jeremiah of foreboding," and says he was "in every way wrong" [1] Hanslick certainly had doubts as to whether the work would ever be quite so successful as the violin concertos of Beethoven and Mendelssohn, but he has a great deal to say in appreciation of the work, and he concludes his notice of it with the sentence: "To sum up, a composition of masterly fashioning and development, but of a somewhat angular invention and of a fantasy, as it were, putting out to sea at half sail."

Specht indeed seems to do his best to belittle Hanslick in his readers' eyes, and the reason is, no doubt, to be found in a remark he makes in speaking about Kalbeck. "I had submitted to him (Kalbeck) with so much faith," he says, "that I afterwards hated

[1] I quote from Mr. Eric Blom's translation.

him for years, for it was his judgment *and that of Hanslick*, accepted by me untested, that caused me to remain for many years without any understanding of Wagner's art, which afterwards became for me the greatest experience and an unequalled intellectual enrichment and possession. I well remember a night in March, when a performance of *Siegfried* for the first time opened up this world for me. I walked about for hours, sobbing, raving, entranced, and filled with a furious resentment against those who had so far cheated me of all this. I believe I should have been guilty of an attempt at murder had I met Max Kalbeck that night, to say nothing of Hanslick." There the true Wagnerite stands revealed with his "unequalled *intellectual* enrichment and possession"! After such a confession we have a pretty good idea of the extent to which Specht was biassed in his attitude to Hanslick. Nevertheless the account which he gives of Hanslick's lectures, which he attended, is an interesting one. They were, he says, "a little disappointing for the reader of his sparkling, accurately formulating and prettily circumstantial featherweight masterpieces of journalism. It was not only that the lectures were fatiguing because of his low and occasionally croaking, though not disagreeable, voice and the curious indifference of his delivery; the content of his course of operatic history was exposed in so bare and colourless a manner in its concision that one could not help growing slack, only to revive when he sat down at the piano to supplement his facts by musical examples. He played everything from memory and it was amusing to see his short, quick fingers scurry across the keys and quite comical to see him trickle out of the keyboard, so to speak, a strongly rhythmic, hopping polka or a merry spruce little piece from a French comic opera, which he did with visible gusto, contentedly and coquettishly skipping with the music. When he spoke of a Bach Passion or of Beethoven's late period, one had the impression that he had to spur himself on and that he felt constrained by an embarrassed reverence to which he lent exceedingly ingenious insight but which nevertheless did not come from his heart." [1] There is a good deal more in this vein. Specht seems unable to withhold a somewhat grudging appreciation in spite of his conviction that Hanslick did not really understand Brahms's music. It would, of course, be too much to say that Hanslick's judgment of Brahms was quite unerring, or that he appreciated to the last detail every aspect of Brahms's writing. But, one may ask, of what contemporary of Brahms could so much be said? The very fact that he knew Brahms well must, as Billroth pointed out in the letter I quoted above, have frequently

[1] *Johannes Brahms*, by Richard Specht, trans. Eric Blom (Dent), pp. 171–172.

made it difficult for him to be sufficiently detached in his attitude, and that is just as likely to have led to an occasional underestimation as to any personal prejudice in Brahms's favour. But it is unnecessary for me to go into details of the relation between Hanslick and Brahms here. It has already been dealt with by most writers on Brahms and Brahms's own letters testify to the high esteem in which he held Hanslick. What impressed him most, as it seems also to have impressed Specht and others, was his honesty and sincerity. The concluding sentence of a somewhat unfavourable notice of Brahms's Double Concerto (a work, by the way, which many Brahmsians still find unsatisfactory, though it seems to me an unqualified success) may be taken as typical of Hanslick's critical attitude. He says, "In Vienna its success was so brilliant that my modest separate verdict, which lays no claim to anything but sincerity, seems indeed already quashed." [1]

[1] *Musikalisches und Litterarisches*, p. 156. This same article contains a sentence significantly omitted from a later version of it printed in *Aus dem Tagebuch*. Speaking of the first movement of the Concerto, Hanslick says, "We are reminded of similar drawbacks in the first movement of the E minor Symphony." In the later version the sentence about his verdict being already quashed is also omitted and a new sentence inserted earlier in the article to the effect that it goes without saying that Brahms has, in any case, made in this work an important addition to music.

CHAPTER XI

HANSLICK AT HIS BEST

IF I had to choose for translation into English a single volume from the dozen or so of Hanslick's collected works, it would be *Musikalische Stationen*. First published in Berlin in 1880, it was designed as part two of *Die Moderne Oper* (Berlin 1875) and bears a dedication dated Vienna, 11 September 1879, "To my dear wife Sophie Hanslick". That is not why I would choose it —although it is possible that Hanslick, who married a young wife late in life, may have been anxious to give the volume a special quality—but because, apart from *The Beautiful in Music*, it contains several substantial essays on matters of genuine historical interest written in Hanslick's best style. The "stations" are in Italy, France and Germany which divide the book into three sections.

The Italian section contains a long article on the singer Adelina Patti, including one of Hanslick's rare "interviews" in quite the modern manner, and also an account of opera and theatre generally in Italy, based on a journey in 1874. The French section has the sub-title "Musical letters from Paris in the year of the Great Exhibition 1878" and contains, in addition to accounts of French operas such as Gounod's *Philémon et Baucis*, and Bizet's *Carmen*, an article on the Rousseau Festival (on the centenary of his death) and one devoted particularly to the acoustics of the Trocadero Hall. Hanslick was present at the first concert in that building and describes in detail the novel experiments that were made in an attempt to plan its acoustical features. "A miniature model was constructed in the same proportions with the greatest accuracy. In it, the curved ceiling over the orchestra was made of a light-reflecting instead of a sound-reflecting, material. It was in fact covered with polished sheet-copper. A light was placed exactly in the middle of the orchestra, where a singer would stand, and care was taken that only the raised rows of seats which would accommodate the audience, were in the path of the reflected rays of light. As a result of this experiment the architects regarded it as necessary to pad all the sides of the walls of the hall so that the sound would be absorbed there. On the other hand, the surfaces of the arched ceiling, under which the orchestra was placed, were made of suitable sound-reflecting material so that it directed the tone to the audience as a mirror reflects light."

Hanslick gives many more details of the experiment but concludes by observing: "The maxim, 'Study how light rays are reflected in a building and you will have discovered the secret of sound waves in that building' sounds good, but the hall that is built on these principles does not." He goes on to quote Charles Garnier, the architect of the Paris Opera who said he left the acoustics of that great building entirely to chance, and believed it was impossible to do otherwise. "Two completely identical opera houses" said Garnier, "built in the same way, turn out to be quite different acoustically." It is little wonder that less skilled architects and musicians tended to accept this argument, and even when Sabine about a quarter of a century later produced results by much more reliable methods—earlier analogies with water and light waves could be shown to be misleading where sound was concerned—it took a long time to produce any reaction in architectural practice.

The section of the book dealing with events in Germany contains a long essay—over fifty pages—on the first performance of The Ring at Bayreuth. Perhaps there are no longer any Wagnerites these days who think of Hanslick as merely a prejudiced, cantankerous or even frivolous critic where Wagner is concerned, but if there are, then these pages are compulsory reading for them. Hanslick goes into great detail about the origin of The Ring and the way in which its composition occupied Wagner for almost twenty-five years. "Whether the work lives up to the expectations of the Bayreuth pilgrims or not, in one respect they will be in agreement—in admiration of the exceptional gifts, energy and capacity for work and agitation, of the man who independently brought this into being and carried it through to final fruition."

He deals with the novel theatre itself and the performances in a painstaking yet entertaining way. He is,
I think, legitimately frivolous about Hans von Wolzogen's thematic guides "a musical Baedeker without
which no respectable tourist dares to go out there ... No
less than ninety Leitmotives are listed by Wolzogen, and
these the wretched festival visitor must impress upon
his memory and be able to sort out and recognise in
the course of four evenings of crowded sound." Of
course we now know this is not really required of the
listener, but in early Bayreuth days it must have been
easy to think that Wolzogen was the authorised guide.
His booklets carried the warning: "Note carefully the
names of author and publisher in view of the appearance of many inferior imitations."

Between the account of Bayreuth and an article on
the first performance of The Ring in Vienna, Hanslick
inserts his one long letter from Wagner part of which
I have quoted in an earlier chapter (P. 11). His description of the performances of the four parts of The
Ring in Vienna—they were not performed as a cycle
but separately over the period 1877-1879—gives some
interesting details. The string section of the orchestra
at Bayreuth, Hanslick tells us, consisted of 16 first
violins, 16 second violins, 12 violas, 12 'cellos and 6
harps. In Vienna there were 14 firsts and 14 seconds,
10 violas, 8 'cellos and 2 harps. But the somewhat
smaller orchestra sounded stronger because it was not

in such a deep orchestral pit as the Bayreuth one. He remarks also on the effectiveness of Hans Richter's arrangement of all the violins "in one compact mass on the left-hand side". This seems to predate considerably the modern custom usually regarded as an innovation of Leopold Stokowski and Sir Henry Wood.

In Vienna the three and a half hours non-stop of *Rheingold* was regarded as too much punishment for opera-goers. "After the first Walhalla scene Wagner's galloping orchestra is brought to a halt with a final chord so that we are not begrudged a ten minute interval ... A theatre is no slave galley, and both musician and listeners are, so to speak, people", as Hanslick delicately puts it. He complains that the rainbow-bridge at the end of *Rheingold* looks too much like a "seven-coloured liver sausage" and wonders if it would not be better to use the technique of "Dissolving-views" (using this English term) by means of projection—which shows that modern productions are not so original as some might like to think.

Musikalische Stationen ends with a perceptive essay on "Grillparzer and Music" in which, largely by means of quotations from Grillparzer himself, Hanslick shows what a large part music played in the poet's life. At the end he says that some may hold against him his reliance so much on Grillparzer's own words. "The less honour due to me, the greater my pleasure in this piece of work." I might say the same about this little vindication of Hanslick, but I will admit I have been glad to see all subsequent publications take note of it, and even more satisfied to read the words with which Professor Friedrich Blume, Editor of the great German dictionary *Die Musik in Geschichte und Gegenwart* concludes his own entry on Hanslick. "It has long been clear", he writes, "that Hanslick's book *Vom Musikalisch-Schönen* opened up a new direction in the consideration of music as an autonomous art, a direction that, leading through Pfitzner, Halm, Kretzschmar, Riemann, Abert, Kurth and others, found its broadest practical realization in today's system of musicology." This is a vastly different conclusion from that indicated by the quotations with which this book began and which, indeed, sparked it off.

BIBLIOGRAPHY

Max Graf: *Composer and Critic—Two Hundred Years of Musical Criticism,* London 1947.

Henry Pleasants: *Vienna's Golden Years of Music 1850-1900.* (extracts from Hanslick's works) New York 1950, London 1951.

The following is a list of Hanslick's works:

1. *Vom Musikalisch-Schönen,* Leipzig, 1854. 9th edition 1896. English translation (from 7th edition) by Gustav Cohen, *The Beautiful in Music,* London, Novello, 1891. The same, edited by Morris Weitz, New York 1957.

2. *Geschichte des Concertwesens in Wien, 2* volumes, Vienna, 1869-70. The second volume has also the title *Aus dem Concertsaal.* Reprinted by Gregg International Publishers Ltd., 1972.

3. *Die Moderne Oper,* 9 volumes, Berlin, 1875 - 1900.
   - I. *Die Moderne Oper*
   - II. *Musikalische Stationen*
   - III. *Aus dem Opernleben der Gegenwart.*
   - IV. *Musikalisches Skizzenbuch.*
   - V. *Musikalisches und Litterarisches.*
   - VI. *Aus dem Tagebuch eines Musikers.*
   - VII. *Fünf Jahre Musik.*
   - VIII. *Am Ende des Jahrhunderts.*
   - IX. *Aus neuen und neuester Zeit.*

Most of these volumes reached several editions. Reprinted by Gregg International Publishers Ltd., 1972.

4. *Suite* — Aufsätze über Musik und Musiker, Vienna, 1885.

5. *Concerte, Componisten und Virtuosen* der letzten 15 Jahre, Berlin, 1886. Reprinted by Gregg International Publishers Ltd., 1972.

6. *Aus meinem Leben,* 2 volumes, Berlin, 1894. Reprinted by Gregg International Publishers Ltd., 1972.

Hanslick also wrote the text for the illustrated works, *Gallerie deutscher Tondichter* (1873) and *Gallerie französischer und italienischer Tondichter* (1874). Apparently this cannot now be traced.

He edited for publication and wrote a preface to. *Wer ist Musikalisch?* by Theodor Billroth, Berlin, 1895.

INDEX